Brian Johnston was one of the best-loved figures on radio and television and will for ever be remembered as 'The Voice of Cricket'. He spent many years with the Outside Broadcasts Department of the BBC, commentating on events such as the Coronation and the Boat Race, before moving on from television to *Test Match Special* for which he was perhaps best known. He also presented 733 episodes of *Down Your Way*. He died in January 1994.

Barry Johnston is Brian's eldest son. In the 1970s he appeared with the harmony group Design on over fifty television shows, before moving to Los Angeles, where he presented the breakfast show on KLOA Radio. He has broadcast regularly on BBC local radio and Radio 5 and now runs BarryMour Productions, who produced *An Evening with Johnners* and *Johnners at the Beeb* as well as recordings with Brian Clough, Donald Sinden, Roy Hudd and many others.

An Evening With

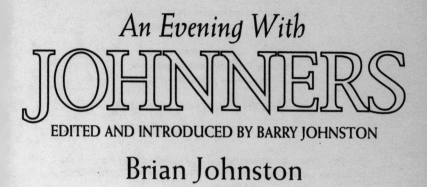

JOHNNERS

EDITED AND INTRODUCED BY BARRY JOHNSTON

Brian Johnston

CORGI BOOKS

AN EVENING WITH JOHNNERS
A CORGI BOOK : 0 552 14494 0

Originally published in Great Britain by Partridge Press,
a division of Transworld Publishers Ltd

PRINTING HISTORY
Partridge Press edition published 1996
Corgi edition published 1997

Set in Times by Falcon Oast Graphic Art

Corgi Books are published by Transworld Publishers Ltd,
61–63 Uxbridge Road, London W5 5SA,
in Australia by Transworld Publishers (Australia) Pty Ltd,
15–25 Helles Avenue, Moorebank, NSW 2170
and in New Zealand by Transworld Publishers (NZ) Ltd,
3 William Pickering Drive, Albany, Auckland.

Reproduced, printed and bound in Great Britain by
Cox & Wyman Ltd, Reading, Berks.

For Fiona, Olivia and Sam.
With love.

Acknowledgements

Grateful acknowledgement is made to Tony Alexander for the use of his letter about the Ian Botham 'Leg Over' incident.

Some of the stories included here can be found in their original versions in the books *Someone Who Was* and *I Say, I Say, I Say* by Brian Johnston and published by Methuen London, Michelin House, 81 Fulham Road, London SW3 6RB.

The recordings of *An Evening with Johnners* and *An Hour with Johnners* by Brian Johnston are available on CD and cassette on Listen For Pleasure and distributed by EMI Records Ltd, EMI House, 43 Brook Green, London W6 7EF.

Contents

The Brian Johnston
Memorial Trust

A charitable trust in Brian Johnston's name was launched in 1995 and its aim is to help cricket at all levels, focusing on young players, village cricket and sports for blind and disabled people, and also to provide support for actors and ex-performers in old age.

For further information please contact:

The Brian Johnston Memorial Trust

PO Box 3897

Lord's Cricket Ground

St John's Wood Road

London NW8 8QG

Telephone: 0171 224 1005

Introduction

In March 1993 I went to see my father at the Hawth Theatre in Crawley. He had just started a nationwide tour of his one-man show *An Evening with Johnners* and was playing to packed houses everywhere he went.

I'd heard most of the anecdotes and jokes at least a dozen times before but I soon found myself laughing out loud along with the rest of the audience. It didn't seem to matter if the stories were familiar or the jokes were corny; in the words of Frank Carson, it was the way he told them!

And no-one told a story like Brian. He would draw you into his confidence as if he'd never told anyone this before, and when he came to the punch-line, he would deliver it with such

3

obvious delight that you couldn't help but laugh, no matter how preposterous the gag.

The show was a triumph and afterwards I thought how wonderful it would be to have a recording of it for posterity, to play to my children in years to come. So I arranged for a recording to be made at the Marlowe Theatre in Canterbury a few weeks later.

As I listened back to the recording, I found myself thinking that it sounded good enough to release as a cassette. Brian was on top form that night and the audience obviously loved him. So I contacted an old friend at EMI Records, who put me in touch with Roger Godbold at Listen For Pleasure, EMI's spoken word label. Roger explained that spoken word recordings generally took a long time to make a profit, but he felt that if we were lucky, we might be able to sell about 5,000 copies in the first year.

Brian was unsure at first. He worried that if people could buy a cassette of all his best anecdotes, then they wouldn't need to buy tickets to see him in person. I managed to persuade him that the laughter on the recording was so infectious that it would make people want to go and see his show even more. In the end he agreed, but I suspect it was more as a favour to me than because he believed it was really true.

The cassette of *An Evening with Johnners* was released in October 1993 and sold more than 5,000 in the first two months! By Christmas it was the number one bestseller in the spoken word chart and it went on to sell more than 100,000 copies in under two years and earned a coveted Gold Disc award. At one point the cassette was selling so fast that it even entered the pop album charts and reached as high as number 46, above stars such as Elton John and UB40!

The sadness was that Brian never lived to see it, because he suffered a heart attack on 2 December 1993 and died peacefully in his sleep just a month later. He was eighty-one.

Brian had been telling all his stories and jokes for years at cricket dinners, ladies' luncheon clubs and hundreds of other charity events and functions. He had developed a number of set speeches, depending on whom he was addressing. He could tell his most famous gaffes, or tales about his colleagues on *Test Match Special*, the royal occasions, *Down Your Way*, or simply collections of jokes – about judges, bishops and even animals.

In the early 1980s Brian's long-time agent, Dabber Davis, had the idea of putting all the stories together into an occasional *Evening with Brian Johnston*. Brian would start by talking for about forty-five minutes and then, in the second half, take questions from the audience. But Brian had so much material that he soon found it easier to talk through the whole show.

One of the first such evenings was at the Sevenoaks Festival. Brian was so used to doing after-dinner speeches that he asked Dabber whether he ought to wear a dinner jacket for the occasion. He laughed when Dabber said that if he did, he would probably frighten half the audience to death! From then on, he always wore a lounge suit.

The evening was a huge success, but in the car on the way home Brian kept asking Dabber, 'Was that all right?' 'Did they like it?' 'Are you sure?' He always wanted to make certain that the audience had enjoyed his performance.

Then in 1992 an old colleague of mine from my music-playing days got in touch with me. Jeff Watts had played bass guitar in the pop group Design with me in the mid-seventies, but now he was a successful promoter and he wondered if my father would be interested in doing a nationwide tour of his one-man show. Brian was intrigued by the idea and said that if Jeff could find any theatres prepared to book him, then he would give it a try.

So Brian made his début with *An Evening with Johnners* at the Chichester Festival Theatre in March 1993. It seats about 1,400 people but the tickets sold out so quickly that they could have easily filled it twice. Brian was amazed.

He had no props. He sat on a high wicker stool, with a table alongside him for his glass of water, and sometimes a vase of flowers. That was it. No notes or lists to jog his memory. Everything was in his head. For two hours he would tell his stories with wit and perfect timing, with no hesitation and no mistakes. It would have been a bravura performance for a comedian or actor of any age, but Brian was then eighty years old. It was a remarkable feat of stamina and endurance.

Brian's old friend John Woodcock, the former cricket

correspondent of *The Times*, went to see him at the Playhouse in Salisbury and told Brian's biographer, Tim Heald, that he buried his face in his hands after hearing Brian's opening lines. 'Wooders' had been hearing the same jokes since 1948! 'He can't tell that one,' he thought, but the audience roared with laughter and he soon realized that there was nothing to worry about. Brian was a natural comedian.

His performance was so relaxed that it never seemed rehearsed, but he was always trying to improve his act. After I saw him in Crawley, the first thing Brian wanted to know was which jokes had worked best. There was one story about Eton which I felt had gone down a bit flat. He agreed and never told it again. He would often call me after a show and be thrilled if a particular story had got a good laugh.

Jeff Watts says that, in the car on the way home, Brian would always go over that night's performance, checking that the audience had enjoyed it or that a new joke had gone well. In quiet moments, Jeff was often surprised to hear what sounded like brass band music, although the radio was switched off. It would be Brian making trumpet noises softly under his breath.

On the way to a show, Brian would frequently drop in for tea with old friends. It made the day seem more like fun than work. He liked to get to a theatre early so that he could get a feel of the stage. He would sit on his stool and chatter away until he felt comfortable. Then he would retire to his dressing room, where he made himself at home, listening to his radio, doing the *Daily Telegraph* crossword and enjoying cups of tea and a plate of biscuits. He was always completely at ease and couldn't wait to get on stage and entertain the audience.

The performance was originally meant to be two halves of forty-five minutes each, but Brian kept adding new stories and soon this had crept up to about sixty minutes each half. When one evening Brian was on stage for more than two hours and twenty minutes, Jeff had to persuade him to keep the show under two hours – otherwise he might have gone on all night!

Normally Brian performed on an empty stage or in front of a curtain, but at the Theatre Royal in Windsor the stage was set up for the following week's performance of the play *The Happiest Days of your Life* starring Patrick Cargill. The set was a school hall with steps leading up to a balcony. Brian was delighted. At the end of his performance he told the audience, 'Thank you very much. Now I'm going up to bed,' and walked straight up the steps and out of sight.

Afterwards Brian would go straight round to the front of house to sign books and autographs and meet the audience. He once joked that he'd signed so many copies of his books that they were now more valuable without his signature! His audiences were usually an interesting mixture of older couples who had been listening to Brian for more than forty years, and younger cricket lovers who knew Brian from *Test Match Special*. He always had time for his fans, even though he wanted to get home after a show, no matter where he was.

Brian loved telling jokes. He would embellish them with lit-tle details that brought them to life. You only have to read his two stories in this book about the Duke of Norfolk to see what I mean. My earliest memories as a child are of my father try-ing to teach me some of his favourite music-hall jokes.

'My car's called Daisy.'
'Why's he called Daisy, Daddy?'
'Because some days he goes and some days he doesn't!'

'My dog's called Carpenter.'
'Why's that, Daddy?'
'Because he's always doing odd jobs about the house. You should see him make a bolt for the door!'

'There were forty men under one umbrella and not one of them got wet.'
'It must have been a jolly big umbrella, Daddy.'
'No, it wasn't raining!'

If he'd been away for a while, Brian would run through all the old jokes to see if I still remembered them. If I got them right he would look as pleased as punch.

He loved to hear new jokes and if they were any good, sooner or later they would find their way into his act. I confess that *I* told him the one about the lady driving up the M1 knitting a pair of socks. I think I saw it in the children's section of my Sunday newspaper. I knew it would make him laugh because it was so simple – and so silly. If Brian heard a new joke that he liked, he couldn't wait to pass it on, although he often couldn't remember from where it had come. A few days after I told him the M1 story he rang me up to tell me his latest joke: 'An old lady was driving up the M1 . . .'!

He would often ring up his close friend William Douglas-Home, the playwright, and before William even had a chance to speak, Brian would say, 'A man went into a pub with a newt on his shoulder . . .' and he was off.

Jeff Watts says that the phrase he remembers Brian saying the most is: 'People are so kind.' In spite of all his years of experience, Brian never got over the fact that people were prepared to leave the warmth of their homes and come out on a cold, wet and windy night and pay to hear him talk for a couple of hours. When members of the public told him how much they enjoyed his show, he was genuinely grateful.

Jeff never saw Brian nervous before a performance, except once, before going on stage at the Richmond Theatre in London. Brian had gone there often as a young man to see some of his favourite comedians but he never dreamed that one day he would appear there himself. On top of that, the theatre had sold out in record time and so he felt a particular responsibility to be at his best.

We recorded the show for a broadcast on Radio 2 – later released as *An Hour with Johnners* – and on the original recording you can hear Brian stumbling over his opening remarks – something he never did – and he sounds a little unsure of himself until he tells the story about the couple celebrating their golden wedding anniversary. Then the audience greets the punch-line with a huge laugh and applause, and you can feel him relax. From then on he gave the performance of his life, and the cassette of *An Hour with Johnners* was nominated for Best Contemporary Comedy in the 1995 Talkies Awards.

He was to perform only one more show. Ten days later he suffered what proved to be a fatal heart attack. In retrospect, he had been overdoing it. After nineteen dates in the spring he had performed another fourteen shows in the autumn, as well as continuing to give after-dinner speeches, commentating on *Test Match Special* and hosting the radio series *Trivia Test Match*, along with all his other engagements.

After Brian's death, the public outpouring of affection was overwhelming. None of the family ever imagined that he would be missed so much. I think Brian had a better idea of how popular he was from the audience reactions he received all around the country, but even he would have been astonished at the front-page newspaper headlines and the glowing tributes on radio and television. The *Daily Telegraph* described him as 'the greatest natural broadcaster of them all.'

And yet it nearly didn't happen. Before the war, Brian had worked for the family coffee business in the City, although he always dreamed of going on the stage as an actor or a comedian. After being demobbed, he was invited to dinner

11

with the BBC war correspondents Stewart Macpherson and Wynford Vaughan-Thomas, whom he'd met while serving in the Grenadier Guards. He told them he was looking for a job in the entertainment world and they put him in touch with the BBC's Outside Broadcasts Department.

Brian passed an audition and joined the BBC on 13 January 1946. He only planned to stay for a few months but was to work for the BBC for the next forty-eight years. His first programmes were live radio broadcasts from music-halls and theatres around the country. Between 1948 and 1952 he presented the live feature *Let's Go Somewhere* on the Saturday night programme *In Town Tonight*. Among his 150 stunts Brian stayed alone in the Chamber of Horrors, rode a circus horse, lay under a passing train, was hauled out of the sea by a helicopter and was attacked by a police dog.

He was one of the first broadcasters to work for both television and radio. In the fifties and sixties he presented children's television shows such as *All Your Own*, *Ask Your Dad* and *What's New*, while on radio he interviewed hundreds of personalities on *Today*, *Meet a Sportsman*, *Married to Fame* and many other series. He also broadcast from the Boat Race for forty-two years.

Brian appeared on dozens of panel games and quiz shows including *Sporting Chance*, *Twenty Questions* and *Trivia Test Match* and commentated on all the major state occasions such as the funeral of King George VI, the Coronation and the Prince of Wales' wedding. He officially retired from the BBC in 1972 but turned freelance and presented *Down Your Way* for the next fifteen years.

Finally, of course, Brian was a cricket commentator on television from 1946 and became the BBC's first cricket correspondent in 1963. After he was dropped by television for telling too many jokes, Brian transferred to radio in 1970 where he became a national institution on *Test Match Special*.

At the age of eighty, Brian achieved his life-long ambition with *An Evening with Johnners* – to get up on stage in front of a sold-out audience and tell jokes, like his music-hall hero, Max Miller. He so enjoyed doing his one-man shows and was thrilled by their success. He told me several times in his last few months that he wanted to give up all the after-dinner speeches and luncheons and concentrate on doing his theatre performances. Sadly, he ran out of time.

Brian used to say he was lucky, but you make your own luck. He loved life and he loved to make people laugh. As you read his words in this book, I hope you can still hear his inimitable voice, chuckling at his own jokes, full of enthusiasm for life, family and friends – and of course, cricket. Then you too will be able to experience the sheer fun and enjoyment of *An Evening with Johnners*.

Barry Johnston
1996

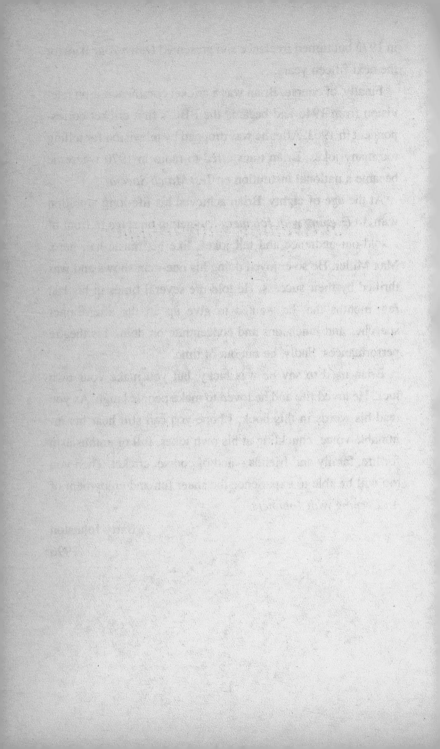

An Evening with Johnners

The stories in this book are taken from the original recordings of *An Evening with Johnners* recorded at the Marlowe Theatre, Canterbury on 25 April 1993 and *An Hour with Johnners* recorded at the Richmond Theatre, London on 21 November 1993. Produced by Barry Johnston and Chris Seymour for BarryMour Productions.

Brian Alexander-O'Neill

MUSIC: *Horseguards, Whitehall* **played by the Sun Life Stanshawe Band.**

The theatre audience hears the familiar sound of a brass band playing the theme tune from the Radio 4 programme *Down Your Way.* **Brian walks on stage to loud applause and seats himself on a high wicker stool.**

Thank you very much.

How nice to be in Canterbury. Although I have to admit, I had to stop myself just now from saying, 'Hello Canterbury.'

I have got into this terrible habit, wherever I am – it can be Bournemouth, Manchester, Birmingham – I say hello to the town and I've got to be very careful, because next week I go across to the Isle of Wight and I'm speaking to the Ladies' Luncheon Club at Cowes!

I am a little bit diffident about speaking to you tonight, for a change, because last week I gave what I thought was the best after-dinner speech I had ever given, but when I had finished a rather drunk chap (at least I hope he was drunk) came up. He said, 'That's the most boring speech I have ever heard in my life.'

And this upset me a bit, but the Chairman of the dinner, who hadn't heard what he said, dragged him away and said to me, 'Don't pay any attention to him – he only repeats what everybody else is saying!'

It's marvellous to see so many people. It must be a very bad night on the telly. You know, you can go to speak and there are very few people. A friend of mine the other day was paid a large fee to go to address what he hoped was a big audience in a town hall. He walked out on the stage and there was one chap sitting in the front row.

Well, he had been paid the fee so he gave the speech, about forty-five minutes, then turned to this chap and said, 'Thank you very much, sir, now I am going.'

And this chap said, 'Please don't go. I'm the second speaker!'

From what I can see of the audience, I am willing to bet that I am the oldest man in the theatre tonight and I am going to warn you about what's going to happen when you get to my age. Three things happen:

First thing is you lose your memory . . .

I can't remember what the other two things are!

But if the ladies will excuse me, I will just tell you what might happen to the men. This is a bit serious really! A friend of mine was celebrating his sixtieth wedding anniversary, his diamond wedding. He and his wife decided to have a second honeymoon – to go to the same town, same hotel, same bedroom, same bed.

They got into bed and the wife put her arms around his shoulders and said, 'Darling, do you remember how romantic you were sixty years ago? You bit me in the neck, you bit me in the shoulder, you bit me in the breast,' and he leapt out of bed and went to the bathroom.

She said, 'What are you doing?' and he said, 'Getting my teeth!'

I have been around rather a long time and it's interesting how sometimes one is recognized and sometimes one isn't. About twenty years ago, coming back from Australia our aeroplane stopped at Bahrain and I walked up and down the transit lounge to get a bit of exercise. An Englishman came up to me and said, 'I think I recognize you, don't I?'

I said, 'Oh, probably,' and reached for my pen. I thought he was going to ask for an autograph.

'Tell me,' he said, 'did you ever drive a bus in Watford?'

I said, 'No.'

'Dead spit of a chap who did,' he said and walked away!

And then, only about two years ago in St John's Wood, where I live, I went to our cleaners and there was a new lady behind the counter, a holiday relief. So I said, 'Can you clean these trousers, please.'

She said, 'Certainly, Mr Johnston.'

I said, 'Very clever of you to recognize me.'

'Oh,' she said, 'I recognized your voice before you even spoke,' if you can work that one out!

And talking of stopping off, I always fly straight back if I go to Australia or anywhere, I don't stop off for a day's rest on the way. But when I was in Australia last time we had a married couple with us and they decided to have three days in Bangkok on the way back. They had two very pleasant days and on the last day the wife said, 'I'm going shopping, you go and amuse yourself.'

He thought, 'Good idea!' So he went to the hotel porter and got the address of a massage parlour. He went and knocked on the door and a little Thai girl came and said, 'What can I do for you, sir.'

He said, 'I'd like a massage.'

'Certainly, sir.'

'How much will that be?'

'A thousand dollars.'

'Oh,' he said, 'I can't afford a thousand dollars. Two hundred dollars is the most that I can afford.'

She said, 'I'm sorry, a thousand is our price. You'd better go somewhere else.'

Well, he didn't bother. He went window shopping and went to pick up his wife at the appointed time. They were walking back to the hotel when down the street came this Thai girl, who looked at his wife and said, 'There you are. See what you get for two hundred dollars!'

I was in India last winter for two of the Test Matches. It is a very strange country. Do you know, I still don't know whether they drive on the left or the right. They steer very well, even round the cows lying in the middle of the road, but it is very frightening.

And, of course, the food is very tricky. But they have got a new dish especially for Englishmen. It's called *Boycott Curry*. You still get the runs, but more slowly!

Now the theme of this evening is really to let you know how lucky I have been in life and how much fun I have had. I started off by having a wonderful family: a mother and father, a sister and two brothers – a very close family.

My wife has put up with me for forty-five years, which is very sweet of her, and we have five lovely children and they have produced seven* grandchildren. And it is, quite seriously,

* Now eight.

very important if you are doing a job like mine, rushing around and meeting a lot of people, to come back to a home in which you know there is love and happiness and comfort. So that's my luck Number One.

I got lucky in my education, because I was sent to the oldest preparatory school in England. The food matched the age of the school! It was in Eastbourne, Temple Grove it was called, and I only remember two things about it really. The matron had a club foot, which was unusual, but the headmaster had a glass eye. It was a very well disguised glass eye and I said to someone, 'How do you know it's a glass eye?'

'Oh,' he said, 'it came out in the conversation.'

I then went to Eton and again I am lucky, because it's the best trade union in Great Britain. There are so many Old Etonians around the place; you meet them and it helps and I have lots of happy memories there.

My late friend, William Douglas-Home, the playwright, did something which amused me. He was sitting an exam and they brought the questions to his desk and one of them was: 'Write as briefly as you can on the future of one of the following subjects.' The first was socialism and the second was coal. So he thought for a moment and chose coal. He wrote one word: 'Smoke.'

And he got seven out of ten, which wasn't bad.

We used to go to a housemaster's house for our history lesson and if the telephone rang in his study he used to say to one of us, 'Go and answer the telephone.' At this time he was very keen on the film actress Anna May Wong. She used to come and have dinner with him and he rather fancied her.

One day the telephone went and he said to this chap, 'Gilliat, go and answer the telephone.'*

Obviously he hoped it was Anna May Wong and when Gilliat came back two minutes later the master said, 'Yes, yes, who was it?'

'Sorry sir,' said Gilliat, 'Wong number!'

That was Eton. Then I went to Oxford, where I read history and P. G. Wodehouse and played cricket about six times a week, which was good fun. And I only achieved one thing there which I don't think anybody else has ever achieved. I actually scored a try at rugby wearing a macintosh. I'll tell you how it happened.

I was playing for New College against Trinity and someone tackled me and pulled my shorts off. I went and stood on the touchline while they went to get another pair and someone said, 'You'd better put this macintosh on to cover your confusion,' which I did.

The ball came down the line and when it got to me on the left-wing I said, 'Outside you!' and took the ball. The referee should have blown his whistle because I hadn't got leave to go back on, but he was laughing so much he just went *pffftt* and couldn't blow and I touched down between the posts!

* Later Sir Martin Gilliat, the Queen Mother's private secretary.

Then, like so many people of that age, I wasn't sure what career I wanted to follow. So I was lucky, in a way, because we had a family business. We used to export coffee from Brazil. We had an office in London and so, reluctantly, I went in there. I didn't understand a thing about coffee. I can confirm there are an awful lot of coffee beans in Brazil but that's about all I can tell you.

I don't think the manager took to me very well. He thought he'd got me one day. I'd had a late night and arrived about ten o'clock and he summoned me to his office. 'Johnston,' he said, 'you should have been here at nine thirty.'

'Why, sir,' I replied, 'what happened?'

And he didn't like that a bit. So it was a good thing for me when the war came and I was able to say to them, 'Sorry, I won't be coming back.'

Again I was lucky, because just before the war began, in about March 1939, some friends and I decided that war was obviously going to come so we ought to try and get into a good regiment.

By a little bit of luck, and the fact that a cousin of mine was commanding the 2nd Battalion at Wellington Barracks, I got in what obviously I think is the best regiment in the British Army – the Grenadier Guards. We had to train every evening. We used to go from the City in our bowler hats and pinstripe suits and march up and down throughout that hot summer,

28

until in the end they said we were qualified to be officer cadets.

When the war came in September this meant we could go straight to Sandhurst to learn how to become officers.

I can never resist making a bad joke, as you probably know, and I tried one out in the first fortnight I was there. They used to have a thing called TEWTS: Tactical Exercise Without Troops, where they took twenty of you out and gave you various military problems to solve.

The officer took us up on a high ridge and said to me, 'Johnston, you're in charge of a section on the top of this ridge and approaching a hundred yards away are a squadron of German Tiger tanks. What steps do you take?'

'Bloody long ones, sir,' I said.

He didn't think that was very funny. I was 'put in the book' for it and had to do a couple of drills, but in the end I passed out from there and got into the Grenadier Guards.

Now when you join the Brigade of Guards it is very strange. You go into the mess and they cut you dead for a fortnight. You probably know half of them, so you try and talk with them but no, they turn away. This is evidently to make sure that new boys don't get too swollen headed.

After a fortnight is up, they more or less look at their watches and say, 'Hello, Brian. Are you here? Have a drink!' and it is all very matey. A bit stupid, I thought, and it happened to me at Shaftesbury when I joined up in 1940.

But at the same time a friend of mine was joining up

down in Sherborne with the Hampshire Regiment and his Commanding Officer treated him completely differently.

'Very glad to have you with us. Want you to get to know people. Want people to get to know you. Monday night we'll have a thrash in the mess. Lots to drink, never did anybody any harm.'

My friend said, 'Terribly sorry, sir, don't drink.'

'Don't worry about that then,' said the Commanding Officer. 'On Wednesday night we'll get a few girls up from the NAAFI and have a bit of slap and tickle in the mess. Great fun. You'll enjoy it.'

My friend said, 'Terribly sorry, sir, I don't approve of that sort of thing.'

So the Commanding Officer looked at him for a moment and said, 'Excuse me for asking, but you aren't by any chance a queer?'

'Certainly not, sir,' said my friend.

'Pity,' said the CO, 'then you won't enjoy Saturday night either!'

So I actually had a very good war with the Grenadiers, and I only mention them, really, because it is thanks to them (or not) you have had to listen to me, if any of you have, since I joined the BBC in 1946. When we were waiting to go to Normandy, two well known commentators from the BBC, Wynford Vaughan-Thomas and Stewart Macpherson, came to brush up on their war reporting, so I got to know them, which was a bit of luck.

I got out of the army in November 1945. I went to a party and I happened to run into them again. Another bit of luck. They said, 'We're very short of people at the BBC because they're still in the services. We want someone in Outside Broadcasts, we know you can talk a bit, come and have a test.' I said, 'I don't want to join the BBC,' but they said 'Come on!' so I said, 'All right,' because I had nothing else to do.

They set me up in Oxford Street, gave me a microphone and said, 'Ask passers-by what they think of the butter ration.' Well, if you ask silly questions you get silly answers, but what they said was, 'It wasn't very good but at least you kept talking. Come and join us for a bit.'

So I said, 'I will, but I shan't stay long.' That was in January 1946 and funnily enough I was with them until I retired as a member of the staff in September 1972, so it suited me, if not everybody who has had to listen to me.

I remember my first broadcast. I'd only been there about a fortnight when they discovered an unexploded bomb in the lake in St James' Park. They drained the lake and there was this huge great sausage of a German bomb and it was announced they were going to blow it up at eleven o'clock one morning and my boss said, 'Right! You can do your first broadcast. You go down there. We'll interrupt the news and you can describe the blowing up of the bomb.'

So we went down with the engineers and we were standing on a little bridge when a policeman came up and said, 'What are you doing?'

I said, 'We're going to commentate on the blowing up of the bomb.'

'Not here, you're not,' he said, 'it's far too dangerous. Go in there.' And he pointed to the ladies loo.

So I went in and stood up on the seat and looked through the louvred windows and I did the commentary from there. I always say I came out looking a bit flushed!

At that time I didn't have anything to do with cricket at all. But I was so happy, because I loved the theatre and my job was to do radio broadcasts live from musicals like *South Pacific*, *Annie Get Your Gun*, *Oklahoma* and *Carousel*. I used to commentate from a box and describe anything visual on stage which the listener might not understand. So I got to know all the stars of all the musicals.

Then every Tuesday we used to go to a music hall and broadcast three acts live from there,* and I got to know all the variety artists such as Arthur Askey, Tommy Trinder and

* *Round the Halls*, 1946.

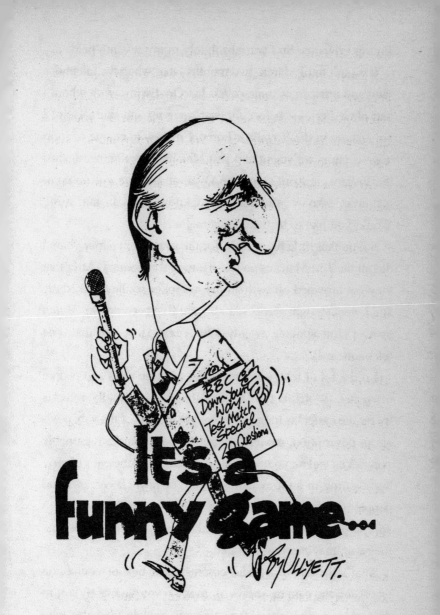

BBC
Down Your Way
Test Match Special
20 Questions
It's a funny Game...
RoyULLYETT.

Ray Ullyett from It's a Funny Game *(W. H. Allen)*

Jimmy Edwards. So I was absolutely in my seventh heaven.

It wasn't until March, two months later, when the telephone rang and a friend of mine called Ian Orr-Ewing, with whom I had played cricket before the war, rang up and said, 'Help! I am just out of the Royal Air Force, I'm now in charge of sport on television, we've got two Test Matches this summer against the Indians, at Lord's and the Oval, and we've got no commentator. I know you can play. I know you can talk a bit. Would you like to be the commentator?'

So, on that little bit of luck, for the next twenty-four years I did all the Test Matches on television in this country. After that they got browned off with all my old jokes so they sacked me and I went straight across to radio and I've been on *Test Match Special* for another twenty-four years. Just on that one telephone call.

I did a lot of television and radio in those days and people often say, 'Which is the easier of the two?' Candidly, radio is by far the easier, as long as you've got the gift of the gab, powers of description, moderately good English and a reasonable voice. You can be yourself but you have to be the eyes of anybody sitting in an armchair at home or in their car, of blind people, or of someone listening on the beach. You've got to paint a picture for them and tell them all you can see, so that they can imagine what it is like.

That's the job of a radio commentator but, of course, on television the camera shows all that, so you've merely got to dot the 'i's and cross the 't's and explain perhaps who someone is if they might not recognize them. You have to edit yourself before you say anything. You think, 'Shall I speak or shan't I?' and that to me is unnatural. We used to have a golden rule which went, 'Only speak when you can add to the picture' and I learnt that the hard way.

In 1954 the Queen and Prince Philip went on a tour of Australia and when they came back the BBC decided to televise their return. They were going to go up as far as the Tower Bridge in the Royal Yacht *Britannia*, get into a launch and travel up to Westminster Pier where they would come ashore and go back to Buckingham Palace in the Irish State Coach.

Before these sorts of events you always talk over with your fellow commentator who's going to say what. Richard Dimbleby was going to be on Westminster Pier, so it was decided that he was going to talk about the people waiting to greet the Queen: the Queen Mother, Princess Margaret, the Lord Lieutenant, the corgis and so on, and he would describe her coming ashore.

But when she got into the Irish State Coach he would pass over to me halfway down Whitehall, where I would be waiting. I would explain all about the Irish State Coach and the Escort, the names of the horses and that sort of thing.

So came the great day and I heard Richard in my headphones just as we'd planned. But as he was beginning to get to the end of his preparation, he looked up the river and said, 'I can't see the Queen arriving yet, it's a bit misty up there. Still, perhaps as we're waiting, I'll tell you something about the Irish State Coach. It weighs thirteen tons, it was given to Queen Victoria, it's made of gold and it is used on state occasions.'

So I was crossing out my notes, as I was listening. Then he said, 'The Queen still isn't here but you might be interested to know the names of the horses. The front one is called Monty, the second one, Eisenhower, and they were given to the Queen by Queen Wilhelmina. Well, it must be the mist up there . . . but anyhow, the Escort today are the Blues in front, commanded by Lieutenant Harcourt-Smith and in the rear are the Life Guards with their white plumes and red tunics . . .' and so on.

I was going mad, crossing things off on my bits of paper. Then he said, 'Ah, here she comes!' and he did all that he was meant to do, and described her coming ashore and the people being presented.

When she got into the coach he said, 'Over to Brian Johnston halfway down Whitehall,' and do you know, the next day people said to me, 'You did the best television commentary I've ever heard. Better than Richard Dimbleby.'

I realized why because, when they came past me, I watched in silence on my monitors as they went into Trafalgar Square, turned left under Admiralty Arch and went about two hundred and fifty yards up the Mall. As they approached Buckingham Palace I said, 'Over now to Berkeley Smith at Buckingham Palace.'

That's all I said! But what else could I say? They knew the Queen, they knew Prince Philip, they knew the horses and the Escort and they knew all about the Irish State Coach. So that was a lesson which I don't think many people follow nowadays, and perhaps they talk too much.

And I learnt another thing from that television time. In 1952 I was chosen to be one of the commentators for the King's funeral, which wasn't quite my cup of tea. I thought, 'Look, you can't get out of it with a joke if you make a mess of things. You must get off to a good start.' So for the first, and the last, time in my life I decided to write out my opening.

I found out that the procession was going to be led by five Metropolitan Policemen mounted on white horses, so I wrote it down. We had about a week before the funeral and I learnt it every night before I went to sleep.

On the day, Richard Dimbleby was in St James' Street. He

described the procession coming past and as it wended its way up Piccadilly and was approaching Hyde Park Corner he said, 'Over now to Brian Johnston at Hyde Park Corner.'

My television producer in my headphones said, 'Go ahead, Brian. Good luck,' and I said, 'Yes, here comes the procession now, led by five Metropolitan Policemen mounted . . .' and on the word 'mounted' I luckily looked up and they *weren't* on white horses.

It was no good pretending they were because at least there was black and white television in those days even if not colour. So very lamely I said, 'Here they are . . . mounted on horse-back.'

My producer, and remember this was a serious occasion, shouted in my ear, 'What on earth do you think they are mounted on? Camels?'

To let you know what sort of thing goes through a commentator's mind, we have an expression we use when describing processions and I had to say to myself, when the cortège came past me, *not* to use it. The expression is: 'Here comes the main body of the procession.'

If I had said it then I should probably have got the sack. But those things do go through one's mind.

The other difference between radio and television is in interviewing. Now, if I am doing a three-minute interview with someone on radio, I'll have a stopwatch. When we get to

38

about two and three-quarter minutes I'll show him the watch, dig him in the ribs or kick him in the shins, and hopefully he'll finish and I can hand back to the studio.

But in television it's very different. If I'm interviewing someone up here, say, for television, the camera will probably be down in the second row and alongside it will be a chap called a studio manager who has headphones on, linked to one of those huge command vehicles. That's where the producer sits and gives his instructions.

He says, 'Right, tell Brian to go ahead,' and you get a signal to start and begin the interview. Then, when he wants you to finish, he gives you a wind-up sign, or if he wants you to go a little longer he signals you to stretch it out a bit. If you over-run, he goes *qweeeck* with his finger across his throat, meaning 'Cut!'

But it doesn't always work. I was doing a programme from an exhibition in the Horticultural Hall and on one of the stands was a jet engine. It was my job to interview a very well-known scientist called Sir Ben Lock-Spicer and in three minutes he had to describe basic things about the jet engine such as what goes in the front and what goes out behind. We rehearsed him and he did it very well indeed.

When they handed over to 'Brian Johnston', I got the signal to go ahead and I said, 'Yes, we've got Sir Ben Lock-Spicer to tell us all about the jet engine,' and he did it absolutely right. When he had finished, as we'd rehearsed, the chap was winding me up very confidently and I said, 'Well, thank you very much to Sir Ben, that was very interesting.'

'Oh,' he said, 'this is *far* more interesting,' and went up to the other end of the engine. The studio manager was now going *qweeeck*, making cutting signs, so I waited for Sir Ben to draw breath and said, 'Well, thank you very much, Sir Ben, we've learnt an awful lot.'

'Oh,' he said, 'you haven't learnt half of it yet,' and went up the other end! The chap was going crazy, going *qweeeck*, *qweeeck*, *qweeeeck*, and we overran. So it doesn't always work. Nowadays they don't worry. They say, 'Sorry, time's up,' and cut someone off in mid-sentence. In those days we tried to be polite.

Another thing is, if you're interviewing someone and they say something which isn't meant to be funny, on radio at least you can hide your smile and hopefully suppress your giggles. On television, if someone says something funny, you mustn't be seen to smile if it's not meant to be funny.

In 1952, when the Indians were here, I was down at Worcester. We always did the first match of the tour on television and inevitably it was raining, as it always did. About lunchtime, my producer said, 'Right, go out under an umbrella and interview the Indian manager. We'll try and fill in some time.'

The Indian manager was a little man called Mr Gupte, a

bit of a volatile little chap. I don't know how much English he understood. Anyhow, I got him under the umbrella and said, 'Mr Gupte, have you got a good team?'

'Oh yes, we've got a very good team.'

'Really,' I said, 'any good batsmen?'

'Seven very good batsmen.'

'What about the bowlers?'

'Six very good bowlers.'

I thought this was getting a bit boring and I'd better try another tack, so I said, 'What about yourself. Are you a selector?'

'No,' he replied. 'I'm a Christian.'

So I pretended not to laugh and said, 'So, tell me about your wicket-keeper . . .'

But I *was* meant to laugh on the occasion when I interviewed Uffa Fox at the Boat Show. Do you remember Uffa Fox? He was the great yachtsman who taught Prince Philip how to sail, a great old sea salt. Sometime before, he'd married a French lady. Nothing very odd about that, except that she couldn't speak a word of English and he couldn't speak a word of French.

So when I was interviewing him at the Boat Show I said, 'Before we talk about the boats, excuse me asking a rather personal question. You married this lady, who doesn't speak your language and you don't speak hers. How does a marriage like that work?'

'Oh,' he said, 'it's quite easy, my dear chap. There are only three things in life worth doing. Eating, drinking and making love – and if you talk during any of them, you are wasting your time!'

A lovely bit of philosophy isn't it?

Now things often go wrong. Sometimes you know they do, sometimes you don't. I'll give you two instances which luckily you didn't know about.

In the late forties and fifties we used to go 'live' in the evenings at about eleven o'clock at night to a wood at Hever Castle in Kent. We used to broadcast the birds singing. If it wasn't raining, the nightingales would sing and so would the other birds.

I used to do this with Henry Douglas-Home, Lord Home's younger brother, who was known as 'The Bird Man'. We would run microphone leads from a van to various parts of the wood and one night at about ten to eleven (remember we were on 'live' at eleven o'clock) he said, 'We've just got time to check the microphones.'

So he asked the engineer, 'Will you bring up the one by the bluebell glade,' and the engineer turned it up and there was a willow warbler, or some other bird.

'Right,' he said, 'that's working. Now, the one by the little bridge by the stream,' and he brought that up and there was a wood pigeon. Then he tried the one by the fir tree and there was a cock pheasant.

Finally he said, 'We've just got time. Let's check up on the one over the rhododendron bush, where we've got the nightingale.'

The engineer brought the microphone up and we heard a girl's voice say, 'If you do that again, Bert, I'll give you a slap in the kisser!'

He just had time to run round and say, 'Please come out.' And a very disgruntled couple came out, doing various things up and saying, 'You might have let us make love in peace.'

He pointed out that in about five minutes time we'd have said, 'Let's hear the dulcet tones of the nightingale,' and goodness knows how far they'd have got by then!

There was another occasion when it was lucky we weren't on the air. I used to do these things in *In Town Tonight* for about three or four minutes each week where I'd do something live and exciting. One of the things we thought we'd do was see what it was like lying under a train.

We found out from Southern Region that, if ever you go into Victoria, about a mile outside the station there are some planks between the lines. If you take the planks up there's a well about three feet deep where the workmen can crouch.

They said I could go in there with my microphone and one of their men and they'd try to get me the *Golden Arrow*. So there I was, and when the studio said, 'Where are you this Saturday night, Brian?' I said, 'I'm lying between the lines outside Victoria Station. We were going to get the *Golden Arrow* but I've just heard it's late and we've got an electric train instead.'

The whole ground shook and I described how the lights from the train were coming towards us. Then the driver blew his horn, because he knew I was there, and the train went over me. It was really such a noise; you wouldn't believe how loud it was. I was having to shout into my microphone.

After it went over me, there were the stars above (we used to do it at night, of course) and I said, 'Well, that's what it's like lying under a train. Back to the studio.'

'Now we can leave,' I said to the man with me, but he said, 'No, you mustn't. The *Golden Arrow* is coming in a couple of minutes and there's a live rail, and with your microphone lead you might trip up. Let's keep still.'

And the *Golden Arrow* did come over us and the reason it was lucky we weren't on the air is because when it went over us, someone was washing their hands – at least, I hope they were! Dreadful! I was absolutely soused.

One story, which you may have heard, was famous. Wynford Vaughan-Thomas was doing the commentary for television when the Queen Mother was launching the *Ark Royal* at Birkenhead. Before it started the producer said, 'Look, I've got three cameras. When we start the broadcast, the first camera will show the Queen Mother breaking the champagne bottle and saying, "God bless all who sail in her." Don't talk during that.

'The next one will show the Marine Band playing, the bunting and the crowd cheering. Don't talk during that. Number three camera will show the chocks coming away and the *Ark Royal* gliding very, very slowly down the slipway. Don't talk during that. But when it reaches the water at the bottom, then go into your commentary.'

It went perfectly. They had a lovely shot of the Queen Mother, then they had the band playing and the bunting, and the chocks coming away. But while the *Ark Royal* was gliding down, the producer happened to look back at his number one camera and he saw the most lovely picture of the Queen Mother waving, as she does.

Forgetting what he had told Wynford, he pressed a button and brought up on the screens at home a close-up of the Queen Mother just, unfortunately, as the *Ark Royal* hit the water.

But Wynford was watching the ship and not his television monitor, so he said, 'There she is, the huge vast bulk of her,' . . . and there was the Queen Mother!

She loved it, of course.

On Mondays of a Test Match at Lord's, the Queen always comes in the afternoon; it normally rains and there's hardly anybody there, but the teams are presented to her during the tea interval. Robert Hudson was doing the commentary when the New Zealanders were being presented to the Queen and he said, 'It's a great occasion for these Commonwealth teams. It's a moment they will always forget!'

Who am I to talk? At the royal wedding of the Prince of Wales and Lady Diana, I was on Queen Anne's statue just in front of St Paul's Cathedral. She was called Brandy Annie, I was told, because she was a bit keen on the grog.

So I had a marvellous view standing there, because all the coaches and carriages drew up about six feet below me. I could see the Queen, with a rug over her knees, being helped out and so on.

I looked over my shoulder and said, 'I can see Lady Diana coming up Ludgate Hill, in her coach with her two escorts. The coach will come below me here, a page will open the door and she will be greeted by her father, Earl Spencer. Then they will walk up the steps together, into the pavilion . . . I mean, Cathedral!'

There are some very good stories about dear old John Snagge. In 1939 John was deputed to go and commentate as the King and Queen left on a trip to Canada. They were going in a big warship called HMS *Vanguard*, from Portsmouth. He was told he had about a quarter of an hour, because the tugs would have to push the ship out, and he was just to describe what was going on.

So he wrote a lot of notes, and read them all out, saying where the voyage was going, where the royal couple were to visit in Canada, the history of the ship and everything. He began to run out of things to say, so he looked around.

'Ah,' he said, 'I can see the King and Queen up there on the bridge. There they are, waving to the crowd. They won't be back for two months. They're saying their farewells.' And he couldn't think of anything else.

'Oh,' he added, 'I see the Queen has gone below now. She's left the bridge and she's gone down below for some reason.' He looked around and still couldn't think of anything to say.

Then, 'Oh yes,' he said, 'I can see water coming through the side of the ship!'

John's a marvellous chap. He's still alive, he's about ninety now. He was the voice of Great Britain. Every big occasion – the Allied landings, Winston Churchill's death, the King's death – he was always the voice they put on the air and he represented us all really.

He was a tremendous announcer in that way, but he didn't

Bill Tidy from Rain Stops Play *(W. H. Allen 1979)*

normally do the sports news. One day he was asked to read it and he got as far as the cricket scores, when he said, 'Yorkshire two hundred and fifty-nine all out. Hutton ill . . . Oh, I'm sorry, Hutton one hundred and eleven!'

He joined the BBC in 1924, and those were the days when Mr Reith had just started the BBC. He became Sir John and later Lord Reith, and was a very serious minded Scotsman, highly religious and very puritan. Everything had to be above board.

He was going round the studios one evening, when he opened the door of a drama studio and, to his horror, he saw one of the producers making love to one of the actresses on a table. He rushed back to his office, summoned his assistant and said, 'I've just seen a producer making love to an actress on a table. Get rid of them both!'

And the chap said, 'You can't, Mr Reith, you can't. It's in the *Radio Times*: the play's going out next week. Think of the scandal.'

Reith thought for a moment and said, 'No, no, you must get rid of them both.'

'But you can't, Mr Reith. You see, she's our best actress and he's our best producer.'

Reith thought for a bit more. 'All right, then,' he said. 'Get rid of the table!'

There's a marvellous story about John Snagge. He did the Boat Race for fifty years. The Boat Race *was* John Snagge. I helped him for about forty years and took over from him in the last nine years, which was great fun.

When you commentate on the Boat Race, you're in a launch and you're always about thirty yards behind the crews, possibly fifty sometimes, if one of them is leading by a lot. So it's very difficult to judge exactly if they are a length up or two lengths up, or whatever it is. But John was always helped when he approached Duke's Meadow, which is on the Middlesex side, before you get to Barnes Bridge.

There were two flagpoles, and there was a man there who had a dark blue flag and a light blue flag, and he used to pull one up, depending on who was in the lead. If Oxford was going ahead, he'd put one flag up, or if Cambridge were drawing level he'd put two together, and so on. Because John was so far behind, he thought this chap must have a far better view, sideways, than he did, so he used to watch the flags.

'Yes,' he'd say, 'I can see the flags there on Duke's Meadow. Oxford are just going up, about a length ahead. No, I see Cambridge are coming up now.' He used to do his commentary from those flags.

When he retired, he had a leaving party given for him and someone said, 'That chap over there is the man who works the flags at Duke's Meadow.'

'Oh,' John said, 'I'll go and talk to him.'

He went over to the chap, who didn't recognize him, and John said, 'Look, you're the man who does these flags. How on earth do you do it? You must have a tremendous knowledge about rowing. You're so accurate, you get the exact distance and everything.'

'Oh,' the chap said, 'it's quite easy. I listen to John Snagge on the radio!'

One other thing about the Boat Race. He and I were on the towpath one Friday before the race. We'd gone to watch the crews, and a lady came up to us and said, 'Oh, do tell me something. I'm very keen on the Boat Race. I've been coming for thirty years and I shall be on the towpath again tomorrow. But tell me one thing. Why are the same two teams always in the final?'

Then, of course, things are said wrong on the air; a lot to do with royalty, funnily enough. Max Robertson once, at the Guildhall, said, 'Here comes the Queen of Norway wearing an off-the-hat face.'

Audrey Russell said, 'The Queen Mother is looking very lovely in dark black,' which is an interesting colour.

Stuart Hibberd was known as 'The Golden Voice', and I think he used to do them on purpose. There was a chap called Ernest Lush, who would play the piano in an interlude if a programme under-ran, and Stuart said once, 'Now there will be an interlush by Ernest Lude!'

They would go to the Pump Room at Bath for chamber music and, inevitably, Stuart said, 'We're now going over to the bathroom at Pump!'

At the opening of Parliament once, they cued over to Henry Riddell, who was one of the commentators, and he said, 'I'm sorry but you're too late. The Queen's just gone round the bend!'

You see, I said an awful lot of stories were to do with royalty, and there are two about them I must tell you.

About twenty-five years ago we used to do a radio programme called *Sporting Chance*. We would go to all the forces all over the world, when we had them then, and on one occasion we were with the Royal Air Force in Germany. We did this sporting quiz with them, and then they asked me if I would like to go round the hospital.

So I went round with the Commanding Officer and talked to the various men and when we came to one ward, the officer said, 'A marvellous thing happened here about four months ago. The Queen Mother came. She went all down the ward, talking to everybody, and she came to a chap who was writing in pain on the bed. She said, "What's wrong with you, my man?"

' "Ma'am, I'm in terrible pain," he said. "I've got the most awful boil on my bum."

' "Ooh," she said, "I hope it doesn't hurt," and was absolutely sweet; never turned a hair and was very sympathetic.

'She passed down the ward, saw the other people and left. And, of course, when she'd gone, the sister came back and gave this chap a tremendous bollocking.

' "How dare you talk like that in front of royalty. Make something up; say you've sprained your ankle, or anything, but never use a word like that again."

' "Sorry, sister," he said, "I realize I shouldn't have done it. I'll never do it again."

'Unfortunately for him, a few weeks later Princess Margaret came out to inspect one of her Highland Regiments. She went down the ward and came to this chap, who was still there, writing in pain on the bed. So she went up to him and said, "What's wrong with you?"

'He remembered what he had promised the sister and he kept his word.

' "Ma'am, I'm in terrible pain," he said. "I've sprained my ankle."

' "Oh," said the Princess, "the boil on your bum is better, is it?" '

You know what happens when a visiting President or King comes to stay at Buckingham Palace. They fly to Gatwick, where the Duke of Kent meets them on the royal train; they come to Victoria and their door opens slap opposite the red carpet.

The Queen greets them and presents the royal family and the Cabinet, and then the Queen and the President go out to the forecourt, where the Queen's company of Grenadier Guards presents arms.

The national anthems are played and the President inspects the Guard of Honour. Then he and the Queen get into an open Victoria carriage and they clip clop back to Buckingham Palace, drawn by six Windsor Greys. Prince Philip and the wife get into the one behind.

This happened some time ago, I'm assured, and all the procedure went exactly as planned: the royal train, the greetings, the bands playing and the Guard of Honour. Then the President and the Queen got into the open Victoria carriage and off went the six Windsor Greys.

The Queen was waving as they went along Buckingham Palace Road, and so was the President, when unfortunately one of the Windsor Greys let out rather a rude noise.

'Sorry about that,' said the Queen.

'Ah,' the President said. 'The honesty of you British. Had you not apologized, I would have thought it was one of the horses!'

The Johnston family, 1985: (left to right, back row) Andrew, Barry, Ian; (middle row) Clare, Brian, Pauline with eldest grandson, Nicholas; (front) Joanna. *Pauline Johnston*

It was the way he told them! Brian giving an after-dinner speech to the Eastleigh Rotary Club, Gloucestershire, 1992. *Homer Sykes/Network*

IN TOWN TONIGHT
Clockwise from top left:

Brian's first *Let's Go Somewhere*
from the Chamber of Horrors at
Madame Tussaud's, 1948.
Graphic Photo Union;

Being shaved and shampooed by the
Crazy Gang in their show *Together
Again* at the Victoria Palace, 1949;

Preparing to broadcast from inside
the letter-box at the main post office
in Oxford, 1951;

Jimmy Edwards struggles to play the
tuba while Brian sucks a lemon
during his act at the Adelphi Theatre.
A. Whittington/John Bull

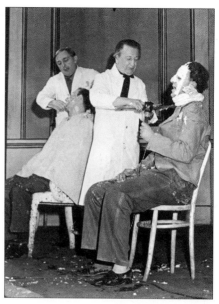

Brian conducts the Sun Life Stanshawe Band as they play the *Down Your Way* signature tune, 1981. Later he used their recording to introduce his stage show *An Evening with Johnners. BBC*

The *Down Your Way* team at Barnstable, Devon, 1982: producer Anthony Smith (left), Brian and sound engineer David Kinrade. *Sandy Porter*

Brian's 733rd and last *Down Your Way* from Lord's Cricket Ground in 1987, with his old friend Denis Compton. *Pauline Johnston*

Brian on the set of *EastEnders* with Mike Read, Jimmy Young and Richard Baker as the voices of Radios 1, 2, 3 and 4 for a BBC promotional film, 1986. *BBC*

Happy birthday cake, Johnners!
75 Not Out in 1987. *Rex Features*

Singing with Norman Cuddeford at an
evening to celebrate the 40th Anniversary of
Sports Report at the London Hilton, 1988.

Brian follows the Queen and the Lord Mayor, Sir Robin Gillett, on the walkabout
from St Paul's to Guildhall on Jubilee Day, 7 June 1977. *Keystone Press*

Brian surrounded by cricket memorabilia in his study at home in St John's Wood, 1989. *Guglielmo Galvin*

Receiving his CBE for services to broadcasting, at Buckingham Palace with his wife, Pauline, and sons, Barry (left), and Andrew, 1991. *Daily Telegraph*

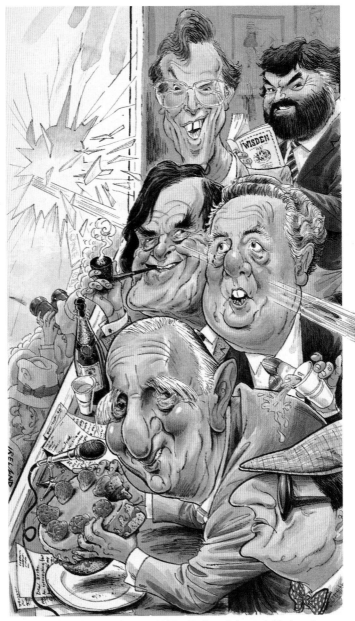

The *Test Match Special* team, 1989. (Left to right, top) Christopher Martin-Jenkins, Bill Frindall; (middle) Fred Trueman, Trevor Bailey; (bottom) Johnners, Henry Blofeld. *John Ireland*

I told you that I used to do these things on *In Town Tonight* when I described the train. This was because *In Town Tonight* in the late forties and fifties was the top programme of them all, including television, because television couldn't be seen outside London until 1950. So there were very few television viewers and there used to be twenty-two million listeners every Saturday night to *In Town Tonight*.

Anybody who was anybody, who came into London – politicians, film stars, businessmen – appeared on the programme. They were interviewed by John Ellison in the studio, but it was all very stilted because the whole thing was scripted. For instance, if a Mrs Smith had done something and was being interviewed, John would say, 'How are you, Mrs Smith?'

'I'm feeling very well, thank you, Mr Ellison.'

'Where do you come from?'

'I come from Hemel Hempstead.'

She read it straight out and it was very dull. So Peter Duncan, the producer, thought they would break this up with a three or four minute 'live' spot in the middle of the programme, either funny or exciting. They asked me to do it, and I did one hundred and fifty of them over four years. It was on most Saturdays and every night was a 'first night', because if it is 'live' – that is, at the time and not recorded – you can't say, 'Sorry. I'll do that again.' You had to get it right.

The very first one was from the Chamber of Horrors at Madame Tussauds. I was given a chair and a very dim light and I sat alone, surrounded by Smith, the Brides in the Bath murderer, Mahon the Trunk murderer and Dr Crippen, and it was terrifying. I was all alone and silent. I tried walking round and the floorboards creaked and something hit me on the head – it was a hangman's rope!

Then, when I went to sit down, I heard a strange noise and I thought it was them but it wasn't: it was the tube running underneath. It was very frightening. I was only there on *In Town Tonight* for four minutes, but I stayed up until midnight. So it was a very eerie experience, and I've never been down the Chamber of Horrors since.

I did all sorts of things. I was very keen on the theatre so I went up on stage with the Crazy Gang during one of their shows. They invited me to take part as the victim in their Barber Shop sketch. I sat down and they poured coloured dyes all over me; they put soap down my mouth and poured water

56

on me. I had to keep talking all the time because the audience were roaring with laughter so much. It made no sense and I could hardly speak with the soap in my mouth, but it was great fun to do.

They were marvellous to work with, except you had to be a bit careful around them. Bud Flanagan was a great, warm-hearted comedian but he did practical jokes all the time. Jack Hylton, who presented their shows, used to go off racing in the daytime. So he always kept a smart city suit hung up in Bud Flanagan's dressing room, and when he came back in the evening he would change into it, before going round the theatres to see his other shows.

Bud had the idea of employing a tailor to come in each day for about a week to take a little bit off the bottom of Jack's trousers and sew them up again. Jack noticed nothing for about four days and then he began to let out his braces until after about seven or eight days he discovered what was going on!

Once I was in Bud's dressing room and he helped me on with my overcoat and said, 'Good night. Nice to have seen you.' The next day, to my horror, as I handed it in at a function at a rather posh hotel, I saw written inside: *This coat has been pinched from Bud Flanagan. Please inform the police at once.*

I did what I think was my favourite broadcast when I wheeled a street piano outside the stage door of the Victoria Palace and by arrangement Bud Flanagan came out. When they cued over to me, he put his hands on my shoulder and together we sang 'Underneath the Arches', which is the only tune I can still play on the piano. That was a great moment, and I don't think there is anybody else alive now who ever sang 'Underneath the Arches' with Bud, because dear old Chesney Allen is dead.

I did funny things like going on the stage when Jimmy Edwards was doing his act with a tuba. I was told that if you suck a lemon in front of people in a brass band, they all dry up. So I asked if he'd mind if I interrupted his act on a Saturday night to see if he could go on playing. Which I did.

I walked out on stage and said, 'Jimmy, I challenge you to go on playing while I suck this lemon.'

'Don't be silly,' he said. 'It's quite easy.'

He started off going (**tuba noises**) – marvellous stuff – and gradually, as I sucked and sucked, he went (**splutter, splutter**) – and he couldn't play. So that worked!

I was the hind legs of a donkey at the London Palladium with Tommy Trinder, and once they put me inside a pillar box. They searched the whole of the British Isles and they found one big enough to take me, outside the Post Office at Oxford. The idea was to help the Post Office at Christmas time and when the letters came through to say, 'Well, that one should have had another stamp on; that one's badly addressed,' and so on.

So I got inside with my microphone and I was talking away and you could hear the noise of the letters dropping in, and when my stopwatch showed that I had got about thirty seconds to go, I said to the listeners, 'I'm just going to stand up now,' and I could hear the clip clop of high heels coming.

I saw a woman's hand about to post a letter and I put my hand out and took it. The poor lady fainted!

I went out in the street, disguised as a tramp, with a hidden microphone and sang 'Tipperary' and 'Pack Up Your Troubles'. That needs a lot of moral courage, to go out in a crowded Strand, as it was on a Saturday night, and start singing. So if I ever see someone singing now, I try to give them something – ten pence perhaps – because I know what they're feeling. In fact, I think I earned about thirteen pennies in three minutes, which wasn't a lot, but it was better than nothing.

I was even hypnotized once, which I won't go into great detail about, but roughly, if you are going to be hypnotized you have to agree that you want to be hypnotized first. This chap got me under and he made me laugh as if I was crazy. I knew I was laughing and I couldn't stop until he clicked his fingers and just said, 'Right. Open your eyes.'

We put it out on the air and it sounded perfectly all right to us but the telephone never stopped ringing with people either saying it was the funniest thing they'd ever heard, or saying it was disgraceful, it was maniacal and the devil had taken hold of Mr Johnston! So that was unfortunate, but it is one of the penalties of doing things 'live'.

One other thing we tried. You know you can see an advertisement in the paper: 'Meet me under the clock at Victoria at eleven o'clock.' Who reads these? Who puts them in? We thought we'd try it out and I knew the Editor of the *Evening News*, so I said, 'Would you put this in on Friday night? Don't tell anybody and we'll see what happens.' The notice was:

Well set-up young gentleman invites young ladies seeking adventure to meet him on the steps of the Criterion Restaurant, Lower Regent Street, 7.15 Saturday night. Identification: blue and white spotted scarf and red carnation. Password: How's your uncle?

I thought we must have a password, because I couldn't believe anyone would come, and at least I could go out and shout, 'How's your uncle?' to passers-by.

So, I'd been doing cricket at Lord's and came down in a taxi about quarter past seven, and said to the taxi driver, 'Hurry up, I'm a bit late.'

He said, 'I can't do anything, Mr Johnston. Piccadilly is very crowded.' So I said, 'Well, I'll get out.' And I made my way through the crowds and into the front of the Criterion and

THE PEOPLE

No. 3628—70th Year

SUNDAY, MAY 20, 1951

- They advertised for girls who wanted "adventure"
- It was a hoax for "In Town Tonight"

B.B.C. STUNT STARTS A
GIRL STAMPEDE
IN PICCADILLY

QUITE THE SILLIEST STUNT THE B.B.C. HAS EVER TRIED CAUSED A STAMPEDE IN PICCADILLY CIRCUS, LONDON, LAST NIGHT. POLICE HAD TO RUSH TO THE SCENE TO CONTROL THE CROWD.

Over five hundred girls started it. They responded to an advertisement in the "personal" column of an evening newspaper asking for "young ladies seeking adventure," to meet there a "well-set-up young gentleman,"

The result—as might have been expected—was alarming.

For not only did the girls turn up in their hundreds, but hundreds of sightseers also rushed to the scene to see what was happening.

With the result that traffic was held up and four police sergeants and eighteen constables were needed to control the jam.

All this was the result of "a lark" by the B.B.C.'s Brian Johnston, who thought it would produce a bit of fun for the "In Town Tonight" programme.

He did it by inserting this advertisement in the personal column of a London evening newspaper on Friday:—

WELL-SET-UP YOUNG GENTLEMAN with amorous intentions invites young ladies seeking adventure to meet him on the steps of the Criterion Restaurant, Lower Regent-st. at 7.15 p.m. Saturday. To be identified by red carnation and blue ... white gloves and grey ... ... words. "How is your uncle?"—Code.

Half an hour before the time announced, the girls began to roll up. Soon there was a stampede.

They began fighting and jostling to get near the steps of the restaurant. Police whistles blew as screaming women were pushed against the windows of near-by shops.

Then a middle-aged woman went down in the crowd and her shoe was stamped on and smashed. A protective circle was formed around her, but still the crowd swelled.

'It's only me'

At 7.21 the "young gentleman" appeared. He had been hiding ... screen inside the restau...

then looked out through the revolving door into Lower Regent Street and it was absolutely jam-packed.

Police were holding everybody back. There were young ladies, some beautiful and some not so beautiful and dotted among the crowd, young men with blue and white spotted scarves and red carnations. I told the listeners, 'This is going to be chaotic, but I've got to go out there and try to interview these ladies.'

So I went out, and there was a loud shout of 'How's your uncle?' and I interviewed some of them and they all swore that they knew nothing about it being a broadcast. They'd wanted to see what this adventure was and, very nice of them, they weren't disappointed that I was neither well set-up, young, or a gentleman.

But it showed that the ad worked and it got an amazing reaction. The *People* the next day had headlines on the front page: 'STUPID BBC STUNT STAMPEDES PICCADILLY' . . . disgraceful Brian Johnston . . . and so on.

So I had my tail between my legs a bit on Monday morning when I went to see my boss, expecting a rocket. 'Sorry,' I said, 'I obviously made a porridge of it.'

'No,' he said, 'they always say we're a staid old Auntie BBC, but as soon as we do something unusual they attack us, so we'll support you, Brian.' So I said, 'Thanks very much,' and left the room.

I had this awful habit then (and I've still got it) of ringing people up and pretending to be someone else. A few minutes after I'd left the room, the telephone rang and my boss picked up the receiver and said, 'Yes.'

And the voice said, 'Inspector Wilson here from West End Central Police Station. I want to complain.' And my boss said, 'Look, Brian, we've had enough of this. Would you mind ringing off.' *Bang!* He slammed the phone down. Of course, the chap rang back about two minutes later and said he really *was* the Inspector!

My son Barry has put a little montage together of four things which I did. The first one is when I went to the circus at Harringay. They had an act where a horse went cantering around, and people from the audience were invited to try and get up on him. They were helped up, to see if they could kneel and then stand on his back and, if they fell, there was a rope they could hold on to.

This went on for about ten minutes and then a clown, who was sitting in the audience disguised as an ordinary member of the public, would always come up and do somersaults and all sorts of things. He always ended his act by pretending to fall off. You see, he was an expert rider and, as he fell, he used to pull a little tape which released his trousers and they always fell off as he landed in the ring.

They said to me, 'Right. You can do that.' So I want you to imagine a packed Harringay Circus seeing a BBC man lose his trousers, and this is what happened:

(**The theatre audience hears a tape recording**)

Ringmaster: 'Ladies and gentlemen, we are now "on the air" and tonight we have a distinguished guest with us, Mr Brian Johnston of *In Town Tonight*, and he's going to have a go.'

Brian: 'Well, here we go. I am approaching the horse. I'll just give him a pat. That's all right. Now, up we go and we are going to try and get up there. Give me a leg up, can you? Whoa! Whoa! No! I'm not up yet!

'Right. I'm cantering around. I'm just sitting up on the horse now and he's going very nicely, a nice steady canter. He's a good horse. And now in a moment I'm going to try and get up on all fours, which is what one has to do, and I'm sitting up . . . Argh! Steady with that whip!

'I'm on all fours now, rather like a cat. I think I'm doing pretty well. But now comes the moment in every circus when you have to stand up on a horse. I'm going to hold on to the rope with one hand, which I'm doing. I'm going to stand up with one leg. I can't get up! I'm standing up. I'm standing up! (**Cheers from the circus audience**)

'Argh! Oh No! (**Roars of laughter**)

'I'm afraid to say my trousers have come off!' (**More laughter**)

Well, they *had* fallen off, and imagine the reaction. It had quite a funny sequel. About a week later, some friends of mine went there, and the clown came out and did his usual act and lost his trousers, like I did. They heard someone behind them say, 'Oh, look at that chap. He's copying what Brian Johnston did on Saturday night!'

Next, I discovered there was a strong lady called Joan Rhodes. She was a smashing blonde, with bristling muscles, but she was very strong. She used to get telephone directories in her stage act and tear them in half – she was huge, with big hands.

I also heard that she could turn someone upside down on the stage and my producer, Peter Duncan, said, 'Well, you'd better go along and see if she can.' So I went on the stage at the Chiswick Empire, with this result:

(**Tape recording**)
Brian: 'Now, I challenge you to lift me now in front of all these people. Will you?'

Joan: 'Here we go then. OK?'

Brian: 'Well now, she is just putting her hand under my knee and she has got her arm round my waist and she's lifting me up . . . . Ooh! Ow! (**Thump**) She's dropped me! We didn't do that in rehearsal. What are we going to do about it?'

Joan: 'Well, as a matter of fact, that one is from Peter Duncan!'

Brian: 'Oh, is it! Thank you very much, Peter. Well now, I'll give you one more chance to do it, and do it properly this time. My kidneys aren't what they were. Right, well now she is doing it again. Her arms are underneath my legs, she's round my waist and my head is down now. I'm looking right up at the ceiling and . . . Oh! (**Sound of money falling on the stage**) All my week's wages have gone! (**Laughter**)

'I'm in a terrible state here. The blood is rushing to my head. Now, can you hold me a bit longer, Joan? I can see the roof up there, the light is shining in my eyes. I absolutely agree you can lift a man of fourteen and a half stone. I plead for mercy. Spare me! Get me up! Help!'
(**More laughter and applause**)

The things people asked me to do! Someone once said, 'Why don't you jump off Nelson's Column, with an umbrella as a parachute?' which I didn't think was a good idea.

One man did make me do something, where I was so frightened you could hear my heart beating like a huge drum. He was called Joe Hitchcock and he was the *News of the World* darts champion for three years running. He used to do an act in a pub with six-inch nails – very sharp. He had a stooge who would stand about six feet away with his back to him and he'd have a cigarette sticking out of his ear. Joe would throw a nail and knock the cigarette out.

Then he'd turn sideways and balance a penny on his nose, and Joe would hit it with the nail. Luckily it wouldn't work on my nose! They challenged me to try and I said I would agree to the cigarette trick. We put the microphone against my heart and it was pounding like mad. Joe missed deliberately once or twice, but he got it in the end. What a mad thing to have done! If he'd missed by just a little, it would have gone through the back of my head. I was absolutely terrified.

After that I found a chap called Mad Johnny Davis. He used to do stunts on motorbikes and he said to me, 'I do a thing where I charge across a field for about a hundred yards and I go through a pyramid of barrels about eight feet high. It's quite safe, I do it regularly. You come on the pillion behind me and we'll broadcast.'

So this is what it sounded like:

(**Tape recording**)
Johnny: 'OK, Brian?'

Brian: 'Yes, all right, Johnny. I've got my head down. I'm leaning forward into Johnny and we are going up about a hundred yards away to have a run at these barrels. We're going up now and I am clinging on and I can promise you it's the most frightening of anything I have done.

'He is just turning round to get into the straight to run at these barrels. I can see them in the distance, a white pyramid, and we're off! We're going off now . . . twenty, thirty miles an hour, I should say. The barrels are coming . . . about ten yards away. Hang on! Here we go . . . (**Crash**) . . . Oohwoah! We're through all right!'

Well, I *was* all right, because I tell you he was an expert. But it was rather frightening.

Finally, because I think it is interesting, it wasn't until 1949 that the lights came up in Piccadilly Circus. They had to repair them, I think, and the LCC said we could broadcast it 'live' on *In Town Tonight* in our Saturday night programme. So I went out on the balcony of the Criterion at Piccadilly Circus and looked down on the crowds all around Eros's statue, and this is what it sounded like:

Brian: 'I expect many of us during the war, when we dreamed of this sight, were cheered up by a certain song called: "I'm going to get lit up when the lights go up in London". Well now, on this balcony with me, not only have we got Hubert Gregg, the chap who wrote it, but on my right, complete in top-hat, white tie and tails, we've got the girl he wrote it for and who sang it. Zoe Gail.

'Now Zoe, you're going to sing the song in a second (**cheers**) – you can hear the crowd now – but just before, we want one or two more lights to come up. Would you like to try a little bit of magic?'

Zoe: 'Oh, I always wanted to be a magician. Now let me think of something original. Hey presto! Abracadabra! Let the lights go up in London!'

(Roar from the crowd)

Brian: 'And, my goodness, it worked! In front of me now I see some of the signs you all know so well. There's a clock over there which tells you it's time for something.* There's a big sign there with eight-foot letters – the oldest sign on the buildings in Piccadilly Circus. The stars are shooting up, there are rockets, different coloured lights, white, yellow, it's marvellous. Well now, Zoe, let's have the song. What about it?'

Zoe: (A piano starts to play) 'Oh, this is the moment I've been waiting for for years.'

(And then she begins to sing: 'I'm going to get lit up when the lights go up in London . . .')

Well, that was quite an occasion and I hope you noticed the

---

* A reference to the Guinness Clock which he couldn't mention as it would mean advertising on the BBC!

little 'deliberate mistake' by the commentator. I said, 'There's a clock there which tells you it's time for something.' What the . . .? It's an interesting point, because that was 'live' and if it had been recorded, they would have said, 'Do it again.' But that went out, so these little slips did occur.

Before we all have a drink, can I just tell you a little bit about *Down Your Way*? This programme ran from 1946 up to 1987, in the format in which I did it. Since then it has changed. But the idea was to go to a city, a town or a village – a hamlet, even – and interview six people. We would find out the history of the place, what it made in the way of industry, any unusual hobbies, the annual ceremonies (if there were any) and all the old traditions and we would talk to the local characters.

It started in 1946 and Stewart Macpherson, the boxing commentator, did the first twelve programmes. In those days, they didn't arrange it with people beforehand, they used to get a list from the Post Office. They did streets in London for the first twelve, and they would look down the list and say, 'We'll go to number five,' or wherever.

After Stewart had done eleven programmes, he was going down one street in London and said, 'Let's try number four – Mrs Wilson,' and knocked on the door of this house. A huge man came to the door and Stewart said, 'Is Mrs Wilson in?'

And this chap said, 'Ah! You're the chap who's been after my missus,' and slugged him one!

So he decided to stick to boxing. It was safer! Then dear old Richard Dimbleby did three hundred of them, until he got too busy on television. After him, Franklin Englemann, whom we called Jingle, took over and he did seven hundred and thirty-three over twenty-two years, which is a long time, but he didn't do every week of the year. He did about forty each year and did other programmes as well.

Alas, he recorded one on a Wednesday afternoon, went back home and died that night. That programme went out on the following Sunday, but they never had any spares. So the next week, someone would have to go and record another programme. And I suppose you could say I was lucky, because I was walking down the corridor at Broadcasting House and someone popped their head out from an office, and said, 'Did you hear about poor Jingle? He's died. Someone's got to record his programme next week. Would you like to do *Down Your Way*?'

Biff

And I did it for the next fifteen years! I did the same number as Franklin Englemann – seven hundred and thirty-three – because I copied exactly what Johnny Francome had done with Peter Scudamore. In 1982, Peter Scudamore was way ahead with the number of winners in the steeplechase jockey table, when he fell off and broke his collar-bone and couldn't ride for the rest of the season.

Johnny Francome gradually drew level with him and one afternoon, when he realized that he had the same number of winners, he threw away his whip and his saddle and said 'I'm not riding anymore – poor old Peter can do nothing about it in hospital. We'll finish level.'

I thought I would do the same with Jingle, because he was up there (**points to heaven**) and couldn't do any more. I chose my last one to be at Lord's and they did me proud. I remember walking into the ground that morning and on the scoreboard was seven hundred and thirty-three Not Out. That's the highest score ever registered on the Grandstand scoreboard. Any cricket buff will know, the highest genuine score was seven hundred and twenty-nine for six by Australia in 1930, when Bradman made two hundred and fifty-four, but mine was the highest!

It was a great programme to do, because you read in the paper about awful things like famine and rape and bombings, and all the stuff which goes on around the world. But if you came round Great Britain with me, as I did for fifteen years, you'd realize what a marvellous nation we are.

Everybody in every place seemed to be doing things for other people; they can be official bodies like the Round Table, Rotary or Lions, but also the Women's Institute, Mothers' Union, Help the Aged, Meals on Wheels – all these people are doing things for other people. It's good news, but it doesn't ever get in the papers. So we are a marvellous nation and I was very lucky to meet so many of them.

I have got one or two favourites. My favourite was someone called Mrs Emily Brewster. She was in Radcliffe-on-Trent and she had just reached a hundred. I went to see her after her birthday and she was surrounded by great grandchildren. I said, 'Did you have a good birthday, Mrs Brewster?'

'Yes, a very good birthday, thank you.'

'Did you get a telegram from the Queen?'

'Yes I did, but I was a bit disappointed.'

'Disappointed?' I said. 'With a telegram from the Queen?'

'Oh yes,' she said. 'It wasn't in her own handwriting!'

I visited a lovely lady in Penkridge in Staffordshire. She was aged eighty-five and still delivering milk every day. She lived in an old farmhouse and she said to me (and this is to me astonishing) that she had never slept a single night of her life outside that house. She had been on a day trip to Great Yarmouth and a day trip to London, but every night she would come back. When you consider how we all rush about the place nowadays and stay away on holidays, that was remarkable.

There was this man down in Usk in Wales. He told me that

at the beginning of the war he was sent to India to look after the mules in a regiment out there. He was a vegetarian, and he knew you don't eat the green stuff if you can help it in India, so he thought he would take some packets of mustard and cress seeds. He took hundreds of packets and after he had had a hot day with the mules he used to take off his wellies, put some mustard and cress seeds in the bottom and go to sleep. And in the morning he would have mustard and cress for breakfast!

I can't help it! That's what he told me and I'm sure it's true.

I interviewed a lovely chap at Biggleswade and he had a ferret down his trousers while I was talking to him. He did give me one big tip. If ever you want to put a ferret down your trousers, make sure it's the male. He's all right, but if it's the female – it's 'gobble time', he tells me!

That's a good tip. You're never likely to do it, but you never know. And I interviewed the rat catcher at Stockport. He was a very well-known rat catcher. He caught all the local rats but if he saw a particularly fine specimen of rat, he would keep it alive, take it to the vet to have it inoculated and put it in a cage in his garden. When I went, there were a hundred brown rats in there. He used to use them for films, for scenes in sewers and so on. While I was interviewing him, a rat was running all over him. Euggh! Awful!

And then, the things people collect. There was a man at Tenterden in Kent who collected prams. He had three hundred and twenty-nine prams in his garden or in his house; two wheelers, four wheelers, some with hoods and some not. I went up to his bedroom and there were prams all in his bedroom too. He said, 'Sadly, my wife has died.' I nearly said, 'Well, I don't blame her!'

Another man in Sussex collected pipes. He had twenty thousand pipes and I saw them all – unbelievable. A man up in Cumberland collected bottles. He had eight thousand bottles of all different descriptions and people came from all over the world to see them.

So you met all these fascinating people and you never really knew if someone was going to tell you a story or not. I interviewed a dentist once, and I said afterwards, 'You didn't tell me a story.'

'No, I had one,' he said, 'but I didn't like to tell you in case it wasn't good enough.'

So I said, 'What was it?'

'Well,' said the dentist, 'an old lady came to have her teeth filled recently and I got the drill up to her mouth but had to withdraw it very quickly. I said, "Excuse me, madam. Do you realize your right hand is gripping me in a very painful place?" And she said, "Yes, we're not going to hurt each other, are we?" '

Finally, someone who did tell me a good story once was the Archbishop of York. I had interviewed him when we did York Minster and I was in his palace at Bishopthorpe, when he said,

'Let's have a glass of sherry and I'll tell you a story.'

'Marvellous,' I thought, 'from an Archbishop.'

'Well,' he said, 'you remember when Our Lord and Moses were negotiating about the Commandments. They went up on to Mount Sinai for seven days and seven nights, working out the Commandments. On the eighth morning, Moses came down the side of the mountain and he said, "Gather round, multitudes, gather round. I've got two bits of news about the Commandments. One good, one bad."

'They said, "Let's have the good news first, Moses."

' "Right," he said, "the good news is, we've got them down to ten," and there was loud applause.

' "What about the bad news?" they said.

' "Oh," said Moses, "the bad news is that adultery is still in!" '

I must tell you one thing which happened. We were going to Brinsworth House in Twickenham, which is where all the old actors and variety artists go in their old age. It is a marvellous place and that is what the Royal Variety Performance is always in aid of. We were going to spend the whole day there and we arrived, going through Richmond, at about ten o'clock.

There was a policeman standing at the crossroads and I said, 'Can you show me the way to Brinsworth House?'

He said, 'Certainly, sir. Go up there, first right, second left, take the right fork, go across the traffic lights and it's up there about two hundred yards on your right.'

'Thank you very much,' I said and, believe it or not, I remembered all that and we got there. We did the programme and finished about four o'clock and came back. When we came through Richmond, the same policeman (I hope he'd had lunch) was standing in the same place. I just couldn't resist it. I wound down my window and said, 'Officer, did you say first left or second left?'

Now, we always asked people for bits of music, which were then slotted in between the interviews, which was why the programme had to be recorded. You couldn't do it 'live', because people always had whatever music they wanted, and we couldn't carry a thousand records around with us. The producer had to go back and find the records at the BBC and then slot them in.

The interviewees always took great pride in what they chose and they always answered very quickly, except for one man, Richard Booth, who was in Hay-on-Wye. If you've never been there, it's on the Herefordshire/Welsh border and it is a book town. Richard started six second-hand bookshops and there are millions of books on any subject you want – bridge, gardening – he has about five hundred books on every topic.

So he was a bit eccentric. He lived in a ruined castle and declared UDI on behalf of Hay-on-Wye and sent out ambassadors to places. He was a bit dotty! Anyhow, I interviewed him about his books and then I asked him for a piece of music. Unfortunately, he caught my eye and got the giggles and took rather a long time to get out what he wanted. Like this:

(Tape recording)
Brian: 'Right, Richard, now we want a piece of music. I don't know what your taste is in that direction?'

Richard: 'I would like ... er, "Golden Years" ...' **(starts to giggle)**

Brian: 'Right, Richard, now we want a piece of music from you. I don't know what your taste is in that direction?'

Richard: (**Laughs**) '... I don't know ...'

Brian: 'Right, Richard, now we want a piece of music from you. I don't know what your taste is in that direction?'

Richard: (**Splutters**)

Brian: (**Now he's got the giggles too**) 'Don't look at me!'

Richard and Brian: (**Both of them speechless with laughter!**)

Brian: 'Right, Richard, now we want a piece of music from you. What's your taste in that direction?'

Richard: 'I would like . . . (**laughs**) . . . Can I have . . . (**more laughter**) . . . Can I . . . (**high-pitched giggles**) . . . Can I have "Golden Years" . . . (**hysterical laughter**) . . . Can I have "Golden Years" or anything by David Bowie.'

Well there you are. He got it out in the end.

And that is the end of the first half. In the second half, if I may, I would like to talk about a game called cricket.

I'm going to refresh myself and I suggest you do too. See you again in about twenty minutes.

Thank you very much.

Interval

While the theatre audience enjoys a quick drink in the bar, we have the chance for a brief interlude with the *Test Match Special* team. Here, as reported exclusively in *Private Eye*, is part of the radio commentary from the legendary Test Match between England and Australia at Headingley in 1981:

Henry Blofeld: 'And we welcome listeners to the World Service with the news that the BBC is about to close it down. Meanwhile here at Headingley the position is that the Australians need only seventy runs to win with nine wickets left. Literally a hopeless task for England, Trevor?'

Trevor Bailey: 'Oh yes, there's absolutely no way that England can win this game now. It's a foregone conclusion.

Australia have got it in the bag.'

Fred Trueman: 'I'll go along with t'that, Trevor – and what's more, I've never seen a worse performance by an England team in all the years I've been associated with the game of cricket, and that's saying something. Wouldn't you agree, Brian?'

Brian Johnston: 'Yes, it's a very sad end to a very disappointing game. As a matter of fact, during the lunch interval I ran into Charlie Badcock who was over here with Bill Woodfull's team in 1934, and old Badders agreed that it was the most disappointing game of cricket he'd ever seen. (**Sound of loud clapping from crowd**) On a lighter note, I'd just like to thank a listener in Pershore, Mrs Elsie Salamander – it is "Salamander", isn't it Fred? I can't make it out.'

Trueman: 'Looks like "Sellotape" to me.'

Johnners: 'That would be a funny name for someone (**laughter**). But anyway, we'd all like to thank the good lady in Pershore for sending us a sample of some really excellent shortcake which she's baked for the Royal Wedding and she's been kind enough to send us a tin of it.'

(More loud applause from crowd)

Bailey: 'I played for the Inscrutables once at Pershore. Lovely little town.'

(More loud applause from crowd)

84

Johnners: 'My wife and I drove through Pershore once on the way to Malvern. I was speaking at the College Speech Day. First-class lunch they gave us, I remember. We bought a dog there.'

Trueman: 'Did I ever tell you what our dog did when t'vicar came to tea?'

Blofeld (laughing nervously): 'Yes, you did, Fred, and I don't think it's entirely suitable for World Service listeners.'

(Huge roar from crowd and chanting)

Bailey (munching): 'Well, I must say that this shortbread is very, very good indeed.'

Johnners: 'And a very handsome tin it's come in. It looks to me like an old Jubilee tin of some sort. Isn't that George V?'

Trueman: 'And I bet it'd fetch a few bob, a tin like that. People will buy any old rubbish these days.'

Blofeld: 'Still, Fred, whatever you say about the tin, I think you have to agree that the shortcake is absolutely first-class.'

(Roaring from crowd now almost continuous)

Johnners: 'By the way, should one say shortcake or short-bread?'

Trueman: 'Up our way, we wouldn't call it t'neither. We call it Parky Loaf, but it comes much thicker than this.'

Johnners: 'Well, that's something for our listeners to write to us about.'

(Thunderous applause from crowd, giving way to deafening cheers, singing, etc.)

Voice in background: 'Mumble, mumble . . .'

Johnners: 'Hang on a minute, Fred, Bill Frindall is trying to tell us something.'

Frindall (for it is he): 'I'm sorry to interrupt, Brian, but I just wanted to point out that England have won by eighteen runs.'

Johnners: 'Thank you, Bill, for that interesting bit of statistical information. Fred, any comment?'

Trueman: 'Well, all I can say is that that was one of the most fantastic bloody pieces of shortcake I've ever eaten in my whole life.'

Bailey: 'Quite. In fact it's what I've been saying all along . . .'
(contd. 94 kHz)

And now, back to the show . . .

Thanks for coming back!

Just before I talk about cricket, can I tell you a story about the Pope. Do you mind?

The Pope went to Ireland about five years ago and his plane was approaching Dublin when it was diverted to Shannon because of crosswinds. Waiting at Dublin to meet the Pope was a glistening white Rolls-Royce, in the charge of a chauffeur called Paddy Murphy.

They got on to Paddy and said, 'Drive like mad to Shannon. The Pope's plane has been diverted and you must be there when he arrives.' So he raced to Shannon, the Pope's plane flew in, and the Pope came down the steps and kissed the ground, as he always does. Then he looked up, and his eyes gleamed when he saw this wonderful white Rolls-Royce. He went up to the driver and said, 'What's your name?'

'Paddy Murphy, your Holiness.'

'Right, Paddy,' said the Pope. 'You get in the back. I'm going to drive.'

So the Pope set off and he was doing seventy, eighty, ninety miles an hour down the narrow Irish roads, when suddenly – '*weeh, wah, weeh, wah*' – a police car signalled him to stop.

'Can I see your licence, sir?' said the policeman.

'Certainly,' said the Pope – he always carries one in his vestments – and handed it over.

The officer said, 'Thank you very much, sir,' and withdrew out of his hearing to ring up his superintendent. 'Super,' he said, 'we're in trouble here. I've found a very, very, very important man's car going at ninety miles per hour. What action am I going to take?'

The super said, 'Well, how important is he? More important than Terry Wogan? Is he more important than the Prime Minister, than royalty?'

'Yes,' said the officer, 'I think he must be.'

So the superintendent said, 'What's his name?'

'I don't know what his name is, but he must be very, very important. He's being driven by the Pope!'

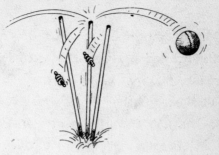

I told you that I did the first twenty-four years after the war on television and I worked with lovely people like Peter West, and Richie Benaud, who came and learnt his trade with us. He learnt very well, didn't he? He's jolly good!

And, of course, dear old Denis Compton. Denis, remember, was the vaguest man there has ever been, and still is. He never remembers a single invitation, never arrives on time, always forgot his box or his bat or his pads, but went out and made a hundred with everybody else's equipment. Very vague and forgetful.

About twenty-three years ago, Middlesex were giving a birthday party for him – his fiftieth birthday. Champagne corks were popping in the Middlesex office up at Lord's when the telephone rang and they said, 'It's for you, Denis.' He went, and came back looking a bit rum.

'Well, who was it, Denis?' they said.

'It's my mother,' said Denis. 'She says I'm only forty-nine!'

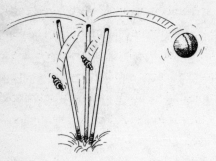

Right, *Test Match Special*. As I've said, I've been lucky all my life, and I was very lucky to get into *Test Match Special*. I did the twenty-four years on the telly, up to 1970, and then they got fed up with all my bad jokes and thought they would get in some Test players to do the commentary – which is very sensible, they do it marvellously. Luckily, I went straight into *Test Match Special* and have been there ever since.

It's a lovely programme to do, because we go and watch cricket like any of you do, with friends. If someone says, 'Have a little drink,' we might have a small one, or if someone tells a good story, we tell it. I hope we never miss a ball, but we have *fun* and that's the great thing to me about cricket.

The remarkable thing is that a lot of our commentary boxes wouldn't pass the Factory Act. They're very hot and stuffy and crowded, and yet I've never seen a single quarrel in one for forty-eight summers and I've never had one. Which *is* remarkable because we're all extroverts – you've got to be to be a commentator – and we're all different.

Of course, the commentary boxes aren't made much better by old Fred* arriving in the morning, smoking an enormous pipe. He fills the box with tobacco smoke! It's a bit better after lunch because he goes round the boxes and has lunch with various people and he always comes back smoking a cigar. We always say his cigars are Adam & Eve cigars – when he's 'ad 'em, we 'eave!

But the great thing is, we do have fun, and we hope we get that fun through the microphone. You can't do this without wonderful people in the box, and I'll tell you about one or two of them.

Sadly, we have lost two very important ones, but one's still going strong – the great Jim Swanton, who, as you know, commentated before the war and even went out to South Africa and did a commentary on the Test Match there. Jim was a marvellous commentator on both radio and on television and a great summarizer, on television especially. Of course, he's written for years for the *Cricketer* and the *Telegraph* and he still writes.

So he's in great form, in his mid-eighties, and he still plays the odd round of golf. His ambition was to be a Second World War golfer – out in thirty-nine, back in forty-five!

On tours, though, he was a wee bit pompous. He used to

* Fred Trueman.

91

stay with Governor-Generals and arrive at the ground with a flag on the car! In fact, when he was on *Desert Island Discs*, Roy Plomley said, 'Mr Swanton, how do you think you would cope with being on a desert island?'

And Jim said, 'It depends who the Governor-General was!'

He's a great talker, and I rang up his wife the other day and said, 'How's Jim?'

She said, 'I haven't spoken to him for about three and a half days.'

'Really,' I said, 'has he been away?'

'No,' she said, 'I didn't like to interrupt!'

He was always very keen on the differential between the amateur and the professional. He thought it was a good thing. But I think he carried it a bit far when he refused to drive in the same car as his chauffeur!

We used to pull his leg unmercifully. I'll just give you two examples.

One happened at Canterbury in 1963, when Colin Cowdrey had hurt his wrist at Lord's and was helping us with the commentary. Peter Richardson was captaining Kent and we arranged with him to pull Mr Swanton's leg. Jim's got quite a deep voice, so we said, 'When we start batting in the morning, and Mr Swanton comes on, we'll wave a handkerchief from on top of our scaffolding.'

So this happened and I was doing the commentary and said, 'I see Peter Richardson is just going up to speak to the umpire. I'll hand over now to Jim Swanton.'

And Jim said, 'Well, I don't know what's going on. He's pointing towards us. It's probably some small boys playing down below. Quite right!'

By arrangement with us, Peter spoke to Bill Copson, the umpire, who then walked towards us. When he was about fifty yards from our scaffolding, he cupped his hands and said, 'Will you stop that booming noise up there. It's putting the batsmen off!'

Of course, Colin said, 'I didn't quite hear that, Bill. Could you say it again?' Poor old Jim!

And the other one was also in the same year, just before that, in 1963 at that wonderful match against the West Indies at Lord's. Do you remember? When Colin came in at number eleven, his wrist in plaster, two balls to go and six runs to win, and with David Allen at the other end. It was a draw, but it was a great match.

Before it started, Jim and I were doing the television and we were told, 'There's 10,000 people in St Peter's Square, waiting for that white puff of smoke which comes out of the Vatican chimney and announces that a new Pope has been elected. If this happens during the Test, we'll leave it immediately and go over to our man in Rome, who'll tell us who the new Pope is.'

So we were waiting for this call to Rome, yapping away, doing the commentary, when out of the corner of my eye I saw the chimney on the Old Tavern had caught fire. Black smoke was belching out, so we got the cameras on to it and I said,

Bill Tidy from Rain Stop Play *(W. H. Allen 1979)*

'There you are. Jim Swanton's been elected Pope!'

He was delighted.

Then there was dear old John Arlott, who died over a year ago now. Very sad. To me, John did more to spread the gospel of cricket than anybody. That marvellous Hampshire burr with the slightly gravel voice, especially in the years after the war, went all around the world, from igloos in Iceland to the outback in Australia.

Every time I heard him, you could smell bat oil and new mown grass, and picture white flannels on a village green with a pub and a church. He could really conjure up cricket for you, and he was very good at painting a picture with words, because before he became a commentator, he was a poet.

To show you how quick he was, and witty, and how well he did it – there was a chap called Asif Masood, who bowled for Pakistan in 1962. Bill Frindall says I once called him Massif Ahsood. (I don't think I did, but never mind!) This chap ran up with bent knees, very low down, and the first time John saw him he said, 'Reminds me of Groucho Marx chasing a pretty waitress!'

John was unique and we miss him terribly. He retired in 1980 and did his last broadcast during the Centenary Test. We knew that he was due to finish at exactly ten to three, and the cameras were there taking pictures of him, and we all thought he'd do a tremendous peroration, saying, 'Thank you for all the years you've listened to me.'

But he got to the end of his over, and when it was time to hand over he said, 'After a word from you, Trevor, it'll be Christopher Martin-Jenkins.'

No more. He got up, walked out and disappeared into the pavilion. Luckily Alan Curtis, on the public address, had heard the broadcast and announced to the crowd: 'John Arlott has just done his last broadcast.'

The Australians were fielding and they all applauded; the crowd stood up and applauded; and Geoff Boycott, who was batting, took his gloves off and clapped! But the interesting thing is that John only came back for one morning of a Test Match in all that time afterwards, to open a stand for Neville Cardus. He didn't ever come back. He stayed down in Alderney, where he wrote books on wine but wasn't very well, sadly, for the last few years. But miss him? Of course we do. He was unique and there will never be another.

We've got one or two eccentric people in the box. What about Blowers – 'my dear old thing' Henry Blofeld? Well, when he was aged eighteen, Henry was one of the best wicket-keepers anyone had ever seen. He was brilliant. He was captain of Eton, and one day he rode a bicycle out of the playing fields at Agar's Plough into Datchet Lane and was knocked over by a Women's Institute bus.

He was lying there in the road, the ambulance took him away and he had an operation on his brain (he got a Blue at Cambridge after that!). But I think that accident gave him what

I call 'busitis', because doing a commentary at Lord's, he said, 'That ball goes through to the wicket-keeper. I can see a number eighty-two bus approaching . . . a Green Line bus . . . a double-decker bus . . .' He had buses on the brain! At the Oval once, he said, 'I can see a good-looking bus!'

At Headingley, he said, 'I can see a butterfly walking across the pitch . . . and what's more, it's got a limp!'

If a pigeon flies by, it's 'a thoughtful-looking pigeon', and he always gets terribly excited: someone dropped an easy catch and he said, 'A very easy catch. Very easy catch. It's a catch he'd have caught ninety-nine times out of a thousand!'

There's Don Mosey, 'The Alderman'. He was talking about David Gower's one hundredth Test Match at Headingley in 1989 and he said, 'This is David Gower's one hundredth Test Match, and I'll tell you something. He's reached his one hundredth Test in fewer Test Matches than any other player!'

Then we have 'The Bearded Wonder', Bill Frindall, the statistician who does all our work for us. He gets up at half past five every morning and enters into his books every single score made the day before, including telegrams that have come in from overseas. He's got details of every single innings played by any first-class batsman. It's a marvellous record, in all these books, so we don't have to do too much homework.

About eight years ago, during the Oval Test, there was a cocktail party to which he was invited, and he went. There was an Arab prince there, in full regalia with the head-dress and white robes, and this Arab prince said to Bill, 'I'll give you fifty quid for your favourite charity, if you dress in my clothes tomorrow and score all day in the commentary box.'

So Bill agreed and the prince went off, changed into a suit and gave Bill the clothes. Next morning, Bill put them on and drove up to the Hobbs Gates at the Oval. On the front of his windscreen it said BBC Radio, and they looked at it and thought, 'Hmmm. Arab? New commentator? Johnston's got the sack, good!' and they let him in.

At the Oval, there is a special space reserved by the back door of the Pavilion, where Bill is allowed to park his car, because he has all these books he has to carry. It is always kept sacred for him. So he drove round as usual, dressed as the Arab, and the steward, seeing an Arab coming into this sacred space, said, 'Sorry, sir. Do you mind backing out? Only Mr Frindall can park here. Do you mind backing out, please sir . . .'

Bill Frindall unwound his window, stuck his Arab's head out and said, 'I've just bought the Oval. I shall park where I bloody well like!'

Of course, this encouraged Fred Trueman to say, 'Anyone know what the fastest thing on two wheels in London is?' and none of us knew. The answer was an Arab riding a bicycle through Golders Green!

I wish I could tell you all Fred's one-liners, but they're not quite suitable. I think I can risk this one because it's very funny actually. About a year ago, he said, 'Johnners? Hear

98

about the flasher who was about to retire?'

I said, 'No, Fred, I haven't.'

'Oh,' he said, 'he's decided to stick it out for another year!'

He told me a clean one last year: 'Johnners,' he said, 'hear about the Pole who went to have his eyes tested? The oculist said, "Can you read that bottom line on the chart?" The Pole said, "Read it? He's my best friend!" '

There are so many stories about Fred, but one which Norman Yardley assured me was true was in about 1949, when Fred was eighteen or so. Yorkshire used to play matches against various clubs, to get fit for the cricket season. Nowadays, people run ten times round the ground or do press-ups, but in those days they used to play cricket to get fit for cricket!

They were playing the Yorkshire Gentlemen once and Fred, very young, virile and tough, bowled very fast bouncers at these poor Yorkshire Gentlemen. Four of them were carried off and went off to hospital. They were twenty-six for six, when out of the pavilion came a very apprehensive-looking figure with grey hair, white bristling moustache, I Zingari cap with a button and a silk shirt buttoned up at the sleeves.

Norman went up to Fred and said, 'Look, this is Brigadier So-and-So, patron of the club. Treat him gently, Fred.' So Fred, who was a very generous man, went up and approached this apprehensive-looking Brigadier with a lovely smile and said, 'Don't worry, Brigadier. Don't worry. I'll give you one to get off the mark.'

The Brigadier's face relaxed in a smile, only to freeze with horror as Fred said, 'Aye, and with second I'll pin you against flipping sight screen!'

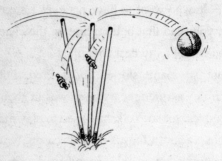

Then we have this funny thing in the box about chocolate cake. It is silly, really, but someone once sent me a cake about sixteen years ago for my birthday and, perhaps unwisely, I said on the radio, 'Thank you very much for that delicious cake.'

Since then, they have come in in droves. We were averaging three or four a day last year! Ray Illingworth's always good for one: he comes in at tea-time. We give some to old ladies' homes and children, we eat some ourselves and we always have about eight visitors in the box (you can hear them chattering often), so we give them some cake.

People take so much trouble. Small boys wait at the back of the pavilion and say, 'My mum's baked this cake for you, Mr Johnston.' It's very touching and they do it beautifully.

They make wonderful cricket scenes in icing on them. I'm

President of a cricket club in Glamorgan – I'm President of about ten different funny clubs – and they come up to Lord's every year with a cake for me. They always present it to me on the Saturday and this year they had a coloured icing replica of a famous picture in Lord's Museum, which shows W. G. Grace batting and a fielder stooping down to field in front of the old stand, where the Warner Stand is now. King Edward VII and Queen Alexandra are seen walking around, with Lillie Langtry, the King's mistress, in the crowd; it's a famous picture.

They did a replica of it in colour. It was marvellous; too good to eat and too good to cut, so we put it in our freezer, and when people came to our house, we didn't say, 'Come and look at this picture on the wall.' We took them into the kitchen! So it is rather stupid but people are kind, and when people are kind you just say, 'Thank you.'

Of course, we played a silly trick on Alan McGilvray a few years ago. Alan is, incidentally, I think the least biased and the fairest of all commentators. He was a very, very good commentator and knew his cricket, because he captained New South Wales in the thirties, when people like Fingleton and O'Reilly were under him, and even Don Bradman on occasion.

So he knew his cricket, but he didn't always understand our jokes. At Lord's, about five years ago, I had cut some cake up into slices on the desk alongside me and I was commentating, when I saw him come in. I pointed to the cake and he nodded, and I went on yap, yapping away and saw him take a slice, and

101

Bill Tidy from Rain Stops Play *(W. H. Allen 1979)*

I said, 'That ball just goes off the edge of the bat and drops in front of first slip . . .'

I saw Alan put it in his mouth and I said, 'We'll ask Alan McGilvray if he thought it was a catch.' He went *pfffft*. There were crumbs everywhere! Silly, really!

I'm lucky at having been on air at great moments like winning the Ashes in 1953, when I was on television at the Oval – 'It's the Ashes! It's the Ashes!' – and again when Ray Illingworth got the Ashes back in 1970/71 in Australia, I was broadcasting back to England.

But luckily for me, I wasn't on when the streaker came on. Remember the streaker in 1975? He came on and did the splits over the stumps. Luckily, John Arlott was on and he did it brilliantly, wittily and gently. He said everything which needed saying; he didn't hide what he could see but he did it in a way I couldn't possibly have done. I'd have got the sack, but he didn't.

There was a Yorkshireman who used to send me rhymes about cricket and he sent me a rhyme, which said:

He ran on in his birthday attire
And he set all the ladies afire
When he came to the stumps
He misjudged his jumps
Now he sings in the Luton Girls Choir!

I often wake up and think, 'Gosh! You've been talking for years about a bit of wood hitting a little bit of leather!' But there are rewards for it. One of the rewards is the reactions that I get from people. Fred and I were talking once about our dogs. He had a big sheepdog called William and I had a little Yorkie called Mini.

He said, 'How's Mini?' and I said, 'I'm very worried about her. We've had to put her in a dog hotel for the first time because my wife's away and our housekeeper's away. When you leave a dog in one of those hotels, they look at you as if to say, "You're never coming back for me. I'm being left!" It's terrible, and I can't get that picture out of my mind. Still, I must go on with the commentary.'

We went on commentating and, about an hour later, there was a knock on the commentary box door. Outside was a man with a dozen red carnations and inside them was a little note saying: 'It's all right. All well here. I know you're coming back for me. Love and licks, Mini.'

A lady in Hounslow had heard me and rung up a florist in Leeds! So that sort of thing makes it worthwhile. All the thousands of letters we get make it worthwhile. They don't always understand us. Some of the letters are marvellous and there are two I always keep on file. Once I said that Freddie Titmus was coming on to bowl and said, 'He's got two short legs, one of them square.'

A woman wrote in: 'No need to be rude about people's disabilities!'

Ken Barrington made a hundred and eleven and I said, 'He's batting very well now. He's a bit lucky – he was dropped when two.' In came a letter saying: 'Mothers should be more careful with their babies!'

And you won't believe this. Once, I was doing a commentary on the annual Whitsun match at Lord's. Middlesex always used to play Sussex, and Middlesex were batting, captained by John Warr. They had made about three hundred for three by tea and I handed back to the studio for the tea interval. They came back to me after tea, 'Over now to Brian Johnston for the latest news at Lord's.'

'Well,' I said, 'the latest news at Lord's is that Warr's declared.' And, you've got to believe it, the BBC duty officer said an old lady rang up to see who it was against!

But you see, it doesn't worry me if I don't make myself understood, because there are other people in this world far higher than me who don't make themselves understood. I'll give you two examples.

Take a judge. You'd think a judge would make himself understood, but this judge was about to sentence a chap who had been found guilty and said, 'Anything you want to say, my man, before I sentence you?'

'Sweet FA, my lord!' said the man.

The judge turned to his clerk and said, 'What did he say?'

'Sweet FA, my lord,' said the clerk.

Tony Hart

'No,' said the judge, 'he definitely said something. I saw him move his lips!'

What about bishops? You'd think bishops would make themselves understood. These two bishops were up at one of these synods in London, where they go to Church House for a different subject each day. They are having a little tea and crumpet in front of the fire at the Athenaeum, working out the subject for the next day and how they're going to deal with it. A difficult one for bishops. Premarital sex.

'For instance,' one said to the other, 'I never slept with my wife before we were married. Did you?'

The other one thought for a moment and said, 'I can't remember. What was her maiden name?'

I must tell you a famous story from the Athenaeum. It's where all the bishops go, and there was a bishop who'd had a very good lunch. He'd ordered a brandy and asked the steward to go to get him some soda. Then he dozed off and was sitting asleep in his armchair when the steward came up and went *Psssttt* into the brandy.

The bishop woke up with a start and said, 'Is that you out of bed again, Millie?'

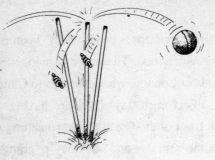

One serious bit of advice. Nothing to do with cricket really, but if you're making a speech at a cricket dinner, or anywhere, and you make a mistake, never stop to apologize. Because if you do, people know you've made a mistake. If you don't apologize and go straight on, people say, 'What did he say?' and, by that time, you're talking about something else.

I've carried this out over my cricket career, because I'm famous for making quite a lot of gaffes. I don't do them on purpose, but in a six-hour day you're bound to make the odd mistake. A lot of them are very old, but I'll tell you one or two.

In 1961 at Headingley, the Australians were fielding and I was doing the television. The camera panned in and showed Neil Harvey at leg-slip, and he filled the screen. Now if you're doing a television commentary and someone fills the screen, you've got to be very quick to talk about him, otherwise the camera goes off and shows something else and you've missed the chance.

Bill Tidy from Rain Stops Play *(W. H. Allen, 1979)*

So without thinking, very hurriedly, I said, 'There's Neil Harvey standing at leg-slip, with his legs wide apart waiting for a tickle!'

I didn't speak for about three minutes after that.

I then went to Hove, for radio, and Sussex were playing Hampshire. Hampshire had a chap called Henry Horton who had a funny stance. When he batted, he more or less stood parallel to the ground, leaned right forward and stuck his bottom out.

I thought I ought to let the radio listeners know, so I said, 'He's got a funny stance, he sticks his bottom out.'

Then I meant to say, 'He looks like he's *sitting* on a *shooting* stick,' but I got it the wrong way round!

When Ray Illingworth was captaining Leicestershire, they came over to me once and I said, 'Welcome to Leicester, where Ray Illingworth has just relieved himself at the Pavilion End!'

At Old Trafford on a Saturday – England against India – it was a dreadful day, pelting with rain and very cold. All the Indian spectators were huddled together in the crowd, looking miserable. Radio Three came over to me, 'Any chance of any play today, Brian?'

I said, 'No, it's wet, it's cold and it's miserable.' I meant to say, 'There's a dirty black cloud,' instead of which I said, 'There's a dirty black *crowd*,' and there they all were!

The most unfortunate one was in 1969 at Lord's where Alan Ward of Derbyshire was playing in his very first Test Match, bowling very fast from the Pavilion End to Glenn Turner of New Zealand.

Off the fifth ball of one of his overs, he got Glenn Turner a terrible blow in the box. Turner collapsed, his bat going one way, his gloves another. The cameras panned in and I had to waffle away, pretending he had been hit anywhere but where he had – as it was a bit rude!

After about three minutes he got up, someone gave him his bat, and I said, 'He looks very pale. Very plucky of him, he's going on batting. One *ball* left!'

Then there was the one that I didn't know I'd said. I'm still not sure whether I did or not! That was after the 1976 match against the West Indies at the Oval, when a lady wrote to me and said:

Dear Mr Johnston,
We do enjoy your commentaries, but you must be more careful, as we have a lot of young people listening. Do you realize what you said the other day?
They came over to you as Michael Holding was bowling to Peter Willey and you said, 'Welcome to the Oval, where the bowler's Holding the batsman's Willey!'

I've digressed a bit! To go back to all these letters, one of the great things for me is the number we get from young boys and girls. They all sign, 'aged eight and a half' or 'aged ten and a half', which is good, because I know how difficult it is now for cricket in schools. But from the number of letters we get, at least they are listening and, I hope, getting an interest in cricket and one day will have a chance to play it.

Sometimes the letters are technical. They want to know about laws, or about cricketers, and we had a wonderful one.

Fred had been going on all afternoon, saying, 'Johnners, cricket is a sideways game. Get the left shoulder over the elbow, a straight bat – sideways on. When you're bowling – sideways – get the swivel action, look over your left shoulder. It's a sideways game, Johnners, a sideways game.'

He went on like this and he was quite right. It *is* a sideways game. About four days later, we got a letter from a young boy, who said:

Dear Mr Trueman,
I was listening to you the other day about cricket being a sideways game. I'm afraid it hasn't worked with me. I'm a wicket-keeper and I let eighteen byes in the first over!

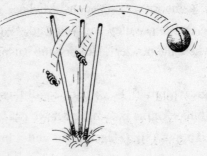

Now, the other thing they do is send me stories and, as you know, I'm a sucker for stories.

They send me stupid riddles: 'Ask Fred what animal he would like to be if he was standing naked in a snow storm.'

'I don't know, Johnners. What animal would I like to be?'

'The answer is: a little 'otter!'

They're terrible jokes: 'What's a Frenchman called if he's shot out of a cannon?'

'I don't know, Johnners.'

'Napoleon Blownapart!'

'Who was the ice-cream man in the Bible?'

'No idea.'

'Walls of Jericho!'

Someone rang in and said, 'What about Lyons of Judah?'

They told me a marvellous story last year, which I enjoyed: There was a lady driving up the M1 – in the middle lane, seventy miles an hour – but knitting at the same time as she was driving. Very difficult. And sure enough, '*weeh, wah, weeh, wah,*' a police car drew alongside her in the outside lane.

A policeman unwound his window and said, 'Pull over!'

'No,' she said. 'A pair of socks!'

Then they told me about the whale, who was swimming along in the Atlantic when he saw his friend the squid, and said, 'Hello, squid. How are you?'

'Ooh, I'm not feeling at all well,' said the squid. 'I'm very ill, not well at all.'

So the whale said, 'Well, get on my back and we'll go and see my friend the octopus.'

They swam along, the squid on the whale's back, and they came to the octopus' house and the octopus said, 'Hello, whale, how are you?'

'I'm fine,' the whale said. 'I've brought that *sick squid* I owe you!'

They told me about the tramp who went to knock on a very imposing house door. A lady came to the door and said, 'What do you want, my man?'

He said, 'I'm very hungry, ma'am. I'd like something to eat.'

'Certainly,' she said. 'Do you like cold rice pudding?'

'Yes, ma'am, I do.'

'Well, come back tomorrow,' she said. 'It's still hot!'

A man went into a pub with a newt on his shoulder and the landlord said, 'That's a nice newt. Who does it belong to?'

The chap said, 'It belongs to me.'

So the landlord said, 'What do you call it?'

'I call it Tiny.'

'Why?'

'Because it's *my newt*!'

Another one!

A man went into a pub and he had a white mouse. He said to the landlord, 'This is an incredible white mouse.'

The landlord said, 'Why?'

'He can play the piano.'

'Don't be stupid,' said the landlord.

'He can,' he said. 'You try him out.'

So he put the mouse down at the pub piano and it tore off a bit of Rachmaninov and some Bach and was absolutely brilliant.

'That's fine,' said the landlord. 'I'll give you fifty quid for him. He can entertain the customers.'

So the man went away and came back the next day with another white mouse. The landlord said, 'Well, what can this one do?'

He said, 'This mouse sings.'

'I don't believe that,' said the landlord. 'No mouse can sing.'

'Well, you try it.'

There was the other white mouse playing the piano, so they put this little mouse alongside the first one and they went through all the Lloyd-Webber songs together and sang them beautifully.

The landlord said, 'That's incredible. I'll give you fifty quid for him too.'

Next morning the man arrived again and the landlord said, 'What have you got for me today?'

The chap said, 'Nothing. My conscience is pricking me. You know that mouse I brought you yesterday that I said could sing.'

'Yes certainly,' said the landlord. 'He's very good.'

'No, he isn't,' said the man, 'the first mouse is a ventriloquist!'

So these letters keep me in touch with the young, which I think is great.

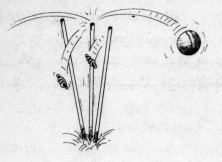

Now you can learn an awful lot from cricket. I've learnt a tremendous amount, and I'll give you some examples. The first example concerns a loveable character and it's to do with drink. It's always dangerous drinking and, in my job, you shouldn't have too much. Although, I am very much in favour of drink, because I think it is sociable, but you mustn't have too much.

Of course, this applies to cricket and dear old 'Hopper' Levitt, W. H. V. Levitt. I'm sure most of you know this story, but I love telling it.

'Hopper' Levitt, a great wicket-keeper, kept wicket once for England against India, but mainly he used to keep for Kent when Les Ames or Godfrey Evans were playing for England. A very good wicket-keeper indeed, he stood up marvellously on the leg side. A great chap. He liked a glass of beer and I think he still does, and he smokes a foul-smelling pipe, but he's a lovely person.

One night, in 1947, he did have rather a heavy night and the next morning he had a most ghastly hangover. He went into the Kent dressing-room and they helped him on with his socks and his boots, his pads, his box and his shirt. Kent were fielding, so they pushed him out onto the field, and a young Kent bowler called Harding (who sadly died, I think, shortly after) – quite a fast bowler – was bowling.

So they put Levitt down eighteen yards behind the stumps. He got down – he couldn't get any lower, his head was throbbing – and the first ball went *pheewwwww* past his right ear. He hadn't moved. Four byes. The next one went *pheewwwww* past his left ear. Four byes. That's eight byes in two balls and he hadn't moved.

The third ball, though, was outside the leg stump and the batsman reached forward and got an outside edge. The ball went very low on the leg side and old 'Hopper' took off and took a most brilliant catch, inches from the ground.

He threw the ball up in the air and went across to the slips and said, 'Do you know, gentlemen, I think that's the first time I've ever caught a batsman off the first ball of the day!'

Now I have checked that story with 'Hopper' and he says there's a *basis* of truth in it!

Anyhow, I think an awful lot of rot is talked about drink. A chap went to a temperance meeting the other day and a man was talking about the dangers of drink. He got two glasses and put water in one, whisky in another. Then he got some worms, put them in the glass of water and they swam around and had a lovely time.

He got some other worms and put them in the whisky, and they shrivelled up and died at the bottom of the glass. He held this glass of whisky up to the chap in the front row and said, 'What, sir, is the conclusion you draw from that?'

The chap thought for a moment, and then said, 'If you've got worms, drink whisky!'

Now, humility. I think humility is very important and I learnt the hard way. I wasn't a bad wicket-keeper, I wasn't a good one. I was just so-so in club cricket, but I loved it and I played an awful lot. After the war – again, how lucky could I be – when I was in the BBC, there was no John Player, Refuge Assurance, Sunday League or whatever it's called now. So you could get all the Test players and all the visiting teams to come and play charity matches on Sunday.

I kept wicket for fifteen years after the war to all the great bowlers – Lindwall, Laker, Lock, Trueman, Miller, Bedser –

you think of any one, I kept wicket. Great fun for me, not much fun for them!

But they were very kind to me. I remember once Jim Laker was bowling, he was absolutely marvellous, you didn't realize what a great bowler he was until you kept wicket. Every ball had tremendous bounce.

So, he bowled a ball and the batsman went right down the pitch and I thought, 'Ah, off-spin bowler – Johnston, get outside the leg stump for a leg-side stumping.'

There I was, waiting, and of course, it was the one which went to the arm and went for four byes, but he didn't mind.

People were kind, but I came down to earth with a bump. I began to think I was getting rather good, playing in these matches, and we went to the Dragon School at Oxford where Richie Benaud, the Australian captain, was playing and I was keeping wicket. He was bowling his flipper and his googly and his top spinner and his leg break. I was reading them all well – they all went for four byes, but I read them well!

Then the last chap came in and Richie bowled him a tremendous leg break. This chap went right down the pitch, missed the ball by *that* much and it came into my gloves with all my old speed, so I thought. I flicked off the bails, just like that, and the umpire said, 'Out!'

A great moment for me, a club cricketer, stumping someone off the Australian captain. So I was looking a bit pleased with myself when I walked off the field and the bursar of the school came up and said, 'Jolly well stumped.'

'Thanks very much,' I said.

'Yes,' he went on, 'I'd also like to congratulate you on the sporting way you tried to give him time to get back!'

Of course, in cricket, if you are a captain you have to have a lot of tact, and being tactful isn't very easy. You have to think very quickly sometimes. A chap the other day was talking to another man and they got on to the subject of Brazil and the first man said, 'Oh, Brazil! It's just a nation of prostitutes and footballers.'

'I'll have you know, sir,' said the other chap, 'my wife was born in Rio de Janeiro and she's a Brazilian.'

The first man thought very quickly and said, 'I was just about to ask, which football team did she play for?'

So that is tact, which you must have as a captain, and leadership is so vital. I've been lucky to commentate with some great captains and two of the great ones, certainly, came from Australia – Bradman, who had a very good side to captain admittedly, except in 1938 – and Richie Benaud, one of the best.

If I pick English captains – Norman Yardley was just too nice to be a great captain, but he was a very good tactician and got the best out of his people and was a great reader of pitches.

Ray Illingworth is my choice for the best all-round captain – determined to win, a great tactician and the men would follow him – he was great.

In later years we've had Mike Brearley; and Graham Gooch, leading from the front – not a great tactician but leading by example, and he certainly worked wonders.

But take Mike Brearley. You see, everybody's different and Mike Brearley, a psychoanalyst, studied the character of each member of his side, to get the best out of them. Tough with one, more gentle with another, so he got the best out of his side. There's a great example of this:

In 1981, that famous match, 'Botham's Match', at Headingley. England had to follow on. Botham hit one hundred and forty-nine not out. Graham Dilley went in and made his first fifty in first-class cricket, in a Test Match, and Chris Old made thirty odd. In the end, England recovered so that Australia had to make only one hundred and thirty to win. Still, they had to make it.

Godfrey Evans, on behalf of Ladbroke's, offered five hundred to one against England, and two people took it. Lillee and Marsh of Australia!

At the beginning of that innings at Headingley, Botham bowled downhill, downwind from the Kirkstall Lane end, took a wicket and was off after about five overs. And trundling upwind and uphill from the Football Stand end was Bob Willis, aged thirty-two then, the fastest man in the side.

Botham came off and Chris Old took over from him. Willis was relieved after about half an hour, and a quarter of an hour later was switched round, came in downhill, downwind and bowled faster and fiercer than I've ever seen him. He took eight for forty-three and England won by eighteen runs.

I remember going up to him afterwards and I said, 'Look, Bob, why did you have to bowl uphill, upwind?'

He said, 'I wondered the same thing. So I went up to Mike Brearley and I said, "Skipper, why am I bowling uphill, upwind?" And Brearley said, "To make you *angry*." '

Now that is captaincy – and it worked!

But there's a different sort of captain I rather like: Keith Miller, the jovial chap from Australia. A marvellous figure of a man. He loved hitting sixes, bowling bouncers and backing horses. He loved women and they loved him. He didn't worry much about tactics or laws, but he just enjoyed playing with his friends on, and off, the field.

There's a lovely story about him. He didn't captain Australia, but he captained New South Wales once, and he was leading them out, walking twenty yards in front, a majestic figure, tossing his hair – I can't toss my hair, but he did.

A chap called Jimmy Burke who, alas, is no longer with us, ran up and tugged his sweater and said, 'Nugget!' (He used to call him 'Nugget') 'Nugget, Nugget, we've got twelve men on the field!'

Miller didn't pause. He went walking on and said, 'Well, tell one of them to bugger off then!'

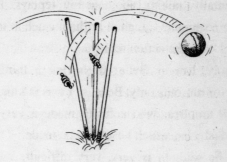

Umpires! I support umpires more than one hundred per cent, if one can do such a thing. I think they do a wonderful job. It's a very difficult one and they have a rotten time these days, especially on television. I hope not so much in club cricket. The dissent shown is awful and the appealing, when it obviously isn't 'out', but they are very much handicapped by this awful thing – the action replay.

In Australia, and they tried it once at Headingley, they show the match on a big screen, and after a decision has been made you can see it replayed on the screen. The wretched umpire has to give a decision in a split second – well, he might take a tiny bit longer, but not much – while the commentators can say, 'Let's have a look at that replay. Hmmm, I'm not sure. Let's have a look from another angle.'

They take about three looks before *they* can decide, so it is unfair on the umpires and I think it makes their task very difficult.

Incidentally, talking about action replays. Did you hear about the Irishman? Caught a brilliant catch at third slip.

Missed it on the action replay!

Seriously, I'm in favour of having a third chap in the pavilion for run-outs only. Because I was talking to one of our first-class umpires, who actually made a very bad run-out decision last year, which he knows he made.

'But,' he said, 'it is very, very difficult. You're standing at square leg, the batsman is coming and you've got to watch for his bat and the popping crease. You've also got to be slightly cross-eyed and watch the stumps to see that the wicket-keeper doesn't mishandle it or that it actually hits the stumps *and* you've got to know, when it hits the stumps, where the bat is!'

It *is* very, very difficult and mistakes are often made, so I'm in favour of run-outs being done on the action replay.

But umpires are treated very badly. I'll tell you two stories which should never have happened. The first one concerns Gilbert Harding. A lot of people remember Gilbert Harding on *What's My Line* – crusty, a brilliant brain, but very intolerant of other people's ignorance. He was a bit rude to them, but he used to send them flowers the next day!

When he was at Ampleforth School he was very short-sighted and very fat, so his headmaster said, 'All right, Harding, you can go for walks instead of playing cricket.'

This infuriated the young master, just down from Oxford, who took the cricket. He thought he would get his own back, which is always dangerous, and when he put the teams up on the board for the Masters against the Boys, underneath he put: Umpire – Gilbert Harding.

So Gilbert had to go and umpire and was not too pleased about it at all. The master went in and hit the boys all around the field. He was ninety-eight not out when a boy, bowling from Gilbert's end, hit him high in the chest and stifled an appeal for leg before wicket. But not before Gilbert had said, 'Out!'

This infuriated the young master who, as he went past Gilbert said, 'Harding! I wasn't out! You weren't paying attention.'

Gilbert thought for a moment and said, 'On the contrary, sir. I *was* paying attention, and you weren't out!'

Then there's the dreadful story which dear, old Jim Laker used to tell about the Commonwealth tour in India in the fifties, under Richie Benaud. There was himself, Bruce Dooland, and George Tribe of Northants, an Australian, who bowled the chinaman – the left arm off-break.

George was getting the batsmen, time and time again, right up against the stumps, palpably out.

'Howzat!'

'Very close, Mr Tribe.'

'Howzat!!'

'Another inch and I'd have had to raise the finger, Mr Tribe.'

'Howzat!!!'

'Nearly, I had to give him the benefit of the doubt, Mr Tribe. Very difficult.'

He was getting fed up with this and off the sixth ball he more or less yorked the chap, who was right in front of his stumps. He *must* have hit the stumps and he turned round and said, 'What about that?'

The man began, 'Mr . . .' and he got no further than that. George turned round, took him by the throat and said, 'Have another look!'

'You're right, Mr Tribe,' he said. 'He's out!'

Well, of course, that shouldn't happen! Then, I always like the original umpire story of village cricket. Where the home umpire, as they were always called, was umpiring against the visiting side. Their best batsman was, again, hit somewhere high up on the chest, there was an appeal for lbw and the local umpire gave 'out' to the home side.

As he went past, this distinguished-looking batsman said, 'I wasn't out, umpire.'

The umpire gave the traditional reply, 'Well, you look in Wednesday's *Gazette* and see.'

This chap said, 'You look. I'm the Editor!'

126

Bill Tidy from Rain Stops Play *(W. H. Allen, 1979)*

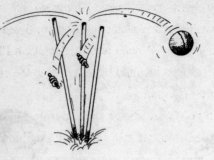

I think kindness is very important. But sometimes it doesn't work out. A lovely story is told about Brian Close. He was the youngest person ever to represent England – eighteen in 1949 – and then he went out to Australia with Freddie Brown as the junior member of the side in 1950/51. I think he made a hundred in his first match and hardly any runs after that – not a great tour for him.

But they were going up by train from Sydney to Newcastle, as they did in those days; it was in the evening and there was a girl sitting in the carriage, nursing a baby.

The chap opposite her kept looking at this baby and she said, 'What are you looking at my baby for?'

'I'd rather not say.'

'What are you looking for?' she went on, and in the end he said, 'All right, I'll tell you. It's the ugliest looking baby I've ever seen in my life!'

128

Well, she rose and burst into tears and she was standing out in the corridor, weeping her eyes out and holding her baby, when the MCC team came along on the way to supper. Bringing up the rear was the junior man, Brian Close, who saw this girl and said, 'What's wrong, dear. Can I help?'

'Yes. I've been insulted by that man in the carriage,' and she burst into tears again.

'I'll tell you what,' Brian said. 'Before I have supper, I'll go along to the restaurant car and bring you back a cup of tea to cheer you up.'

She said, 'Oh, please,' and burst into tears again.

He came back two minutes later and she was still crying. 'There you are, dear,' he said, 'a cup of tea to cheer you up. And what's more, I've also brought a banana for the monkey!'

Brian Close was undoubtedly one of the bravest cricketers I've ever seen. Remember him batting against the West Indies in 1963, against Hall and Griffiths? Rather than risk giving a catch, he bared his breast at them and let the ball hit him; you could see the maker's name all over him. He was very brave and, of course, he always fielded near in at short leg.

There's a story about when Yorkshire were playing Gloucestershire and Martin Young was batting; Ray Illingworth was bowling and Close was right in there at forward short leg.

For once, Ray bowled a bit of a short ball outside the off stump, which Martin Young pulled and he got Close right above his right eye. The ball ballooned up over Jimmy Binks, the wicket-keeper, and into the hands of Phil Sharpe at first slip – caught!

Blood was pouring down over Close's face. It didn't worry him, he just wiped it away, and fielded there for about another ten minutes. Then the lunch interval came and he walked back – blood pouring down – and as he went in, one of the members said, 'Mr Close, you mustn't stand as near as that. It's very dangerous. What would have happened if it had hit you slap between the eyes?'

He said, 'He'd have been caught at cover!'

He's a great person, and one of the great characters.

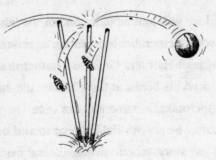

A bit of advice which I give to people – sometimes it will get you promotion and sometimes the sack – is, if you are going to do something which you think is the right thing to do, but you suspect your boss may not think so, I say, stick to your principles and do it.

There's a lovely cricket story, which is an old one now, but it illustrates this perfectly, about the late Duke of Norfolk, who went as manager of Ted Dexter's team to Australia in 1962/63. A strange chap to have as a manager, a Duke, but they loved him in Australia – they called him 'Dukey' – because wherever MCC played he leased a racehorse and ran it in the local meeting.

They told me this story, which I hope is true. MCC were playing against South Australia at Adelaide, and about twenty-two miles outside Adelaide there is a racecourse called Gawlor. There's a lovely paddock there with eucalyptus trees and gum trees, very picturesque.

The Duke had a horse running there, so he thought he would go and see it. He spotted it under the eucalyptus tree and walked across the paddock in his pinstripe suit, panama hat and MCC ribbon, very much the Duke. As he approached the horse, to his horror, he saw the trainer put his hand in his pocket and give the horse something to eat.

He thought, 'Oh, my God. I'm a member of the Jockey Club at home,' and went up to the trainer and said, 'I hope you didn't give him anything you shouldn't have, trainer. We don't want any trouble with dope here.'

'No, no, Your Grace,' said the trainer, 'I just gave him a lump of sugar. I'm going to eat one myself. Would you like one too, Your Grace?'

The Duke thought he'd better humour him, so he ate the lump of sugar, talked about the race and went off to watch it from the Grandstand. Five minutes before the race started, in came the jockeys, waddling as they do.

The Duke's jockey went up under the eucalyptus tree to his horse and the trainer said, 'Look. This is a seven-furlong race. The first five furlongs, keep tucked in behind and don't move. But for the last two furlongs, give him all you've got, and if anyone passes you after that, it's either the Duke of Norfolk or myself!'

But the story about doing what is right or what is wrong concerns one of those marvellous matches at Arundel, which the Duke used to run against local teams. He was running one against Sussex Martlets and they had an eleven o'clock start in those days. At a quarter to eleven they were an umpire short, so the Duke said, 'All right. I'll go down to the Castle and get my butler, Meadows.'

So he got in his shooting brake with the labrador lying in the back, drove down to the Castle and went through the green baize door into the pantry. There was Meadows the butler, polishing the coronets and the silver. The Duke said, 'Meadows, take your apron off, put a white coat on and come and umpire.'

So, reluctantly, Meadows did, although he didn't know much about cricket. It was one of those days of gentle drizzle, not wet enough to stop, but making the ground very slippery

Bill Tidy from Rain Stops Play *(W. H. Allen, 1979)*

and difficult. The Duke's team were batting, one hundred and ten for eight, and the Duke came in at number ten and went to the non-striker's end. The chap batting thought, 'I'd better let him have the bowling,' so he pushed one to cover and said, 'Come on, Your Grace, come one.'

His Grace set off, but he slipped up and landed flat on his face in the middle of the pitch. Meanwhile cover point picked the ball up and threw it over the top of the stumps. The wicket-keeper whipped off the bails, turned to the square leg umpire and said, 'How's that?'

The square leg umpire, inevitably, was Meadows the butler. What was he to do? He knew what he ought to do and there was his boss, who wouldn't be too pleased, but he stuck to his principles.

He drew himself up to his full height and said, 'His Grace is not in!'

Apropos of that, when I was in Australia with Peter May's team, there was an umpire who wasn't very good. His name was McInnes and on the previous tour with Len Hutton he had been very good indeed, but somehow he had failed. He made one or two bad mistakes.

Tom Crawford used to captain Kent 2nd XI and was a great friend of mine, and he was talking to Don Bradman about this. 'The trouble with your umpires, Don,' he said, 'is that they've never actually played Test cricket or even Shield cricket. They're not first-class cricketers. They've learnt all the laws and passed exams, but they don't know what goes on in the middle. At home all our umpires are either Test players or County players.' (That was true then, but I think we've got about four now who aren't.)

Don got very indignant about this. 'No, no,' he said. 'What about McInnes? He played for South Australia until his eyesight went.'

Then he realized what he'd said!

Now, I'm going to lunch at The Savoy on Wednesday with the Australian team, and I shall tell them the story which was told by the best after-dinner speaker I ever heard, the late Lord Justice Birkett. He told it in 1953 to Lindsay Hassett's team and said how welcome they would be wherever they went in the British Isles.

'But,' he said, 'one word of warning, we don't wear our hearts on our sleeves in this country. We are a bit cool and reserved; we often don't know the chap next door, even though he's lived there for forty-five years. But don't worry, on the surface we may not be friendly, but underneath it we are. Indeed, we treat each other exactly the same.'

He then told the famous story of the Flying Scotsman leaving Kings Cross non-stop to Edinburgh. Four men were reading papers in the corner of a carriage. They glided through the Hertfordshire countryside and after thirty-two miles, got to Hitchin. One of them put down *The Times* that he was reading and said, 'Look, we've got three hundred and eighty-four miles to go. Let's talk and get to know each other and the journey will go so much more pleasantly. I'll tell you about myself. I'm a Brigadier, I'm married and I've got one son who's a banker.'

The chap sitting opposite him put down his copy of *The Times* and said, 'You won't believe this. I'm also a Brigadier, I'm married and I've got a son who's a schoolmaster.'

The third chap said, 'Well, this is the most amazing co-incidence,' and he put down *his Times*. 'I'm a Brigadier, I'm married and I've got a son who's a lawyer.'

They all looked at the fourth chap, who was reading *the Sun*, and they said, 'What about you?' He said, 'I'd rather not,' so they went on talking amongst themselves.

They got to a little place called Sandy, about fifteen miles up the line, and they turned to this chap and said, 'Come on, join in. We're having so much more fun.'

He said, 'No, I don't want to.'

'Come on,' they said, 'be a sport.'

'All right, have it your own way,' he said. 'I'm a Regimental Sergeant Major. I am NOT married. I've got three sons – and they are all three Brigadiers!'

There are other things about cricket: we're told there's a lot of pressure these days, and people do get irritated, aggravated and frustrated but I think it's dreadful, because, as I say, it should be fun.

A father I knew was trying to teach his boy the right way to play cricket and he said, 'Never get irritated.'

The boy said, 'What's irritation, Dad?'

So the father said, 'Well, I'll teach you about irritation, aggravation and frustration.' He got a telephone and dialled a number at random and a man's voice said, 'Hello?'

'Is Alf there?' said the father.

'No,' said the man, 'Alf doesn't live here,' and *bang* he put the phone down.

The father said, 'That man is a bit irritated, son.'

'What about aggravation, Dad?'

'All right,' he said, and dialled the same number again.

The man's voice said 'Hello?' and the father said, 'Is Alf there?'

'No, Alf isn't here! Are you the same man who rang just now? If you don't ring off, I shall get the police!' *Bang*.

'He's very aggravated now, son,' said the father.

'Yeah, but what about frustration, Dad?'

So the father dialled the same number. The man's voice said, 'Hello?'

The father said, 'It's Alf here. Have there been any calls for me this morning?'

The other thing is: don't panic. There's nothing more awful than seeing a cricket team panicking. I love Corporal Jones in *Dad's Army*: 'Don't panic! Don't panic!' and there's a perfect example of how not to panic:

A chap woke up one morning, drew his curtains, looked out

of the window and saw, to his horror, a gorilla in a tree in his garden. Well, he didn't panic, because he went straight to the *Yellow Pages*, dialled a Gorilla Catcher and said, 'I've got a gorilla in my tree.'

'No problem, sir, I'll be round in quarter of an hour.'

A quarter of an hour later, a little yellow van arrived and out of the back of it the gorilla catcher took a ladder, a pair of handcuffs, a shotgun and a bull-terrier. So the chap said, 'What are all these things for?'

'Oh, it's quite easy,' said the gorilla catcher. 'I put the ladder against the tree, I climb it and shake it. The gorilla will then fall to the ground. Now, at that point, I want you to release the bull-terrier, who is trained to bite human beings and gorillas in a very painful place.

'The gorilla knows this and, to save himself, will put his hands down over his private parts. You run forward, put the handcuffs on him, and you've got him.'

'That's all right,' said the chap, 'but what about the shotgun?'

'Oh, said the gorilla catcher, 'I forgot to tell you about the shotgun. Sometimes, when I climb the ladder and shake the tree, *I* fall down. In that case, get the shotgun and shoot the bull-terrier!'

Now there's one more story that my young ten and a half years old grandson, Nicholas, told me. It's extraordinary the stories they come back with from school!

This was about three football fans, an Englishman, a

Scotsman and an Irishman. They were stranded in the desert. I don't know what they were doing in the desert, but they'd been there for a week. They were very hungry and they came across a dead camel, so they decided to cut it up and eat it.

The Scotsman said, 'I support Hearts. I'll eat the heart.'

The Englishman said, 'Well, I support Liverpool. I'll eat the liver.'

The Irishman looked a bit glum. He said, 'I support the Arsenal. I'm not feeling very hungry!'

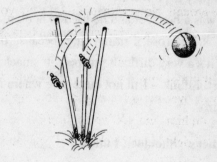

Just before we stop, I've said cricket is fun. Now, I want you to cast your mind back to August 1991, the Friday of the Oval Test Match against the West Indies. Bad light stopped play at half past six and Peter Baxter, our producer, turned to Jonathan Agnew and myself and said, 'Go through the scorecard, will you please, to fill in time.'

Gallantly, I started the scorecard. I got down as far as Ian

Botham, who had been out 'hit wicket' and this is what followed:

(Tape recording)

Johnners: 'Botham, in the end, out in the most extra-ordinary way.'

Aggers: 'Oh, it was ever so sad really. It was interesting, because we were talking and he had just started to loosen up. He had started to look, perhaps, for the big blows through the off-side, for anything a little bit wide – and I remember saying, "It looks as if Ian Botham is just start-ing to play his old way."

'It was a bouncer and he tried to hook it. Why he tried to hook Ambrose, I'm not sure, because on this sort of pitch it's a very difficult prospect. It smacked him on the helmet, I think – I'm not quite sure where it did actually hit him . . .'

Johnners: 'Shoulder, I think.'

Aggers: 'Shoulder, was it? As he tried to hook, he lost his balance, and he knew – this is the tragic thing about it – he knew exactly what was going to happen. He tried to step over the stumps and just flicked a bail with his right pad.'

Johnners: 'He more or less tried to do the splits over it and, unfortunately, the inner part of his thigh must have just removed the bail.'

Aggers: 'He just didn't quite get his leg over!'

Johnners: 'Anyhow, (**chuckle**) he did very well indeed, batting one hundred and thirty-one minutes and hit three fours.' (**Aggers beginning to giggle in the background**) 'And then we had Lewis playing extremely well for forty-seven not out . . . Aggers, do stop it . . . and he was joined by DeFreitas who was in for forty minutes, a useful little partnership there.

'They put on thirty-five in forty minutes and then he was caught by Dujon off Walsh.' (**Aggers starting to titter**) 'Lawrence, always entertaining, batted for thirty-five . . . (**Johnners starts to wheeze**) . . . thirty-five . . . (**gasping**) . . . minutes . . . hit a four over the wicket-keeper's h . . . (**high-pitched giggle**) . . . Aggers, for goodness sake stop it . . . he hit a f . . .' (**uncontrollable laughter**)

Aggers: 'Yes, Lawrence . . . (**complete collapse**) . . . extremely well . . .'

Johnners and Aggers: (**Both now helpless with laughter.**)

Johnners: (**In hysterics**) '. . . He hit . . . (**his voice getting higher and higher**) . . . he hit a four over the wicket-keeper's head and he was out for nine . . . (**crying with laughter**) . . . and Tufnell came in and batted for twelve minutes, then was caught by Haynes off Patterson for two . . . **(calming down)** . . . and there were fifty-four extras and England were all out for four hundred and nineteen . . . I've stopped laughing now . . .'

That was the most professional piece of broadcasting I ever did! You see, I kept going regardless. Peter Baxter said to Aggers, 'Say something, Aggers! Say something!' He was meant to join in, but he got as far as, 'Lawrence . . .' and he burst out laughing too.

But it does show that cricket is fun and the nice thing is, the BBC put it on *Pick of the Week* and they also put it out on television on the BBC *Sport Personality of the Year* programme. I'm often interviewed by people from abroad and they always mention it, so the giggle went round the world, and I don't think it was a bad thing.

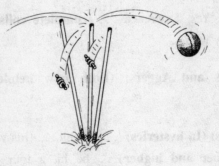

Can I once again thank you very much for coming. I hope you have enjoyed meeting me, I have enjoyed meeting you. So I will finish on this little song, which goes like this:

Columbus discovered America
Hudson discovered New York
Benjamin Franklin discovered the spark
Which Edison discovered would light up the dark

Oh, Marconi discovered the wireless telegraph
Across the ocean blue
But the greatest discovery
Was when you discovered me
And I discovered you.

Thank you very much.

THE END

And finally . . .

When the famous Ian Botham 'Leg Over' incident was originally broadcast, I was listening to *Test Match Special* on the radio at home. As soon as I heard Brian's first stifled chuckle, somehow I knew he was going to get a fit of the giggles. By the time he finally stopped, I was crying with laughter myself and had tears running down my face. It was, and still is, the funniest thing I have ever heard.

Thousands of others felt the same. Many drivers, listening in their cars on the way home from work, had to pull into the side of the road until they had stopped laughing. There were reports of a three-mile tailback at the entrance to the Dartford Tunnel on the M25, because several drivers queueing for the toll-booths were laughing so much they were unable to carry on!

A few days after the broadcast, the following letter was received by the BBC's Head of Litigation from a Mr Tony Alexander, a solicitor in Milton Keynes. I have spoken to Mr Alexander and, happily, all involved are now fully recovered from their injuries:

Dear Sir,

Re: Cricket Commentary – Friday 9 August 1991.

We have been consulted by Mr Wally Painter and his wife Dolly. On Friday evening our clients were in the process of redecorating their hallway. Mr Painter was perched on a ladder in the stairwell of his house, whilst Mrs Painter held the ladder steady. Our clients' aquarium with assorted tropical fish was situated at the foot of the stairwell.

Our clients are keen cricket enthusiasts, and were listening to the summary of the day's play on Radio Three, when Mr Brian Johnston and Mr Jon Agnew were discussing Mr Ian Botham's dismissal, which apparently involved some footwork which Mr Botham failed to consummate.

The ensuing events caused a vibration in the ladder and, in spite of Mrs Painter's firm grasp, Mr Painter fell off the ladder, landing awkwardly on the partial landing, thereby dislocating his left wrist. The ladder fell on Mrs Painter, who suffered a contusion to her forehead.

The 5 litre drum of Dulux Sandalwood Emulsion fell and crashed through the aquarium, which flooded the hallway, depositing various frantically flapping exotic fish onto a Persian rug. The Painters' pedigree Persian cat (Mr Painter spent many years in Tehran as an adviser to the late Shah) grabbed one of the fish, a Malayan red-spined Gurnot, and promptly choked to death.

The water seeped down into the cellar where the

electricity meters are located. There were several short circuits, which resulted in (a) the main switchboard being severely damaged and (b) the burglar alarm (which is connected to the local police station) being set off.

Meanwhile, Mr and Mrs Painter were staggering towards the bathroom, apparently in paroxysms of hysterical laughter despite their injuries. Within minutes, the police arrived, and believing the Painters to be vandals and suspecting, as both were incoherent, that they had been taking drugs, promptly arrested them.

We are now instructed to inform you that our clients hold the Corporation (BBC) liable for:-

(a) Their personal injuries.

(b) The loss of the aquarium and various exotic fish collected over several years.

(c) The damage to the Persian rug.

(d) Damage to the electrical installation and burglar alarm.

(e) Death of the cat.

However, they are prepared to settle all claims for damages in respect of the above provided that you supply them with a recording of the discussion with Mr Johnston and Mr Agnew, together with an undertaking from Mr Johnston and Mr Agnew that they will not in future discuss Mr Botham's footwork or lack of it, while Mr and Mrs Painter are decorating their property.

I am happy to report that Mr and Mrs Painter received their tape.

SUMMERS WILL NEVER BE THE SAME
A Tribute to Brian Johnston
Edited by Christopher Martin-Jenkins & Pat Gibson

'I understand there are some men who do not like cricket, but I
would not like my daughter to marry one'
Brian Johnston

Brian Johnston, who died in January 1994, was one of the best
loved figures on radio. His unique broadcasting style won him
a special place in the hearts of listeners everywhere.

Although 'Johnners' became known as the voice of cricket, he
was also a national figure as the presenter of *Down Your Way*.
His many other broadcasting credits include presenting for
television the Queen's Coronation and the Boat Race.

Most of all, Johnners will be remembered for his schoolboy
humour. Specially revised and updated for the paperback edition, this volume of tributes includes anecdotes and memoirs
from over sixty colleagues and friends – including John Major,
Sir Colin Cowdrey, Richie Benaud, John Paul Getty, Lord
Whitelaw, Tim Rice, Lord Carrington and Jonathan Agnew –
as well as short extracts from Johnners's own publications and
transcripts of some of his most famous broadcasts.

0 552 99631 9

BEATING THE FIELD
My Own Story
by Brian Lara with Brian Scovell

On 18 April 1994 at the St John's Recreation Ground in
Antigua, Brian Lara scored 375 against England for the West
Indies, smashing the Test record set in 1958 by Sir Gary
Sobers. On 6 June of the same year, he scored an unbeaten 501
against Durham at Edgbaston, beating Hanif Mohammed's
record of 499. In eight first-class innings, he scored seven
centuries. He is now indisputably the world's number-one
batsman.

Beating the Field is Brian Lara's own story of his record-
breaking career so far, one in which he has already achieved
more than most cricketers do in a lifetime. The second
youngest of a family of eleven, Lara reveals the philosophy that
has taken him from the back streets of a small village, Santa
Cruz, in Trinidad, to the cricketing heights.

Critical of county cricket and many of its regulations, Lara
writes frankly about the behind-the-scenes dramas at
Warwickshire as he helped them to a record-breaking season
unparalleled in English cricket. He also gives his trenchant
opinions on some of cricket's recent controversies. *Beating the
Field* provides a unique insight into the mind of the biggest
name to emerge in cricket for many years, a man whose ambition, as he told his sister Agnes when he was eight, was 'to
become the greatest cricketer there has ever been.'

0 552 14350 2

A SELECTED LIST OF SPORTS TITLES AVAILABLE FROM CORGI AND PARTRIDGE PRESS